W9-BYZ-801

How to Get an

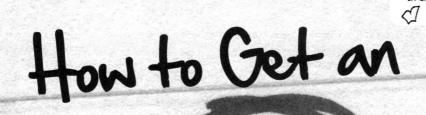

A+

in Spanish

William C. Harvey, M.S.

BARRON'S

About the Author: Bill Harvey has been helping students of all ages to learn Spanish for over 30 years. His shortcuts, tips, and secrets to studying Spanish are specifically designed for anyone interested in learning how to communicate, instead of struggling through traditional classroom instruction. You can find out more about Bill, including the titles of his many Barron's books, simply by searching William C. Harvey, M.S., on the Internet.

Barron's Licensing Agreement/Disclaimer of Warranty

1. **Ownership of Rights.** The MP3 disc in the plastic sleeve was created for Barron's Educational Series, Inc., and the editorial contents therein remain the intellectual property of Barron's. Users may not reproduce the disc, authorize or permit the disc's reproduction, transmit the disc, or permit any portion thereof to be transmitted for any purpose whatsoever.
2. **License.** Barron's hereby grants to the consumer of this product the limited license to use same solely for personal use. Any other use shall be in violation of Barron's rights to the aforesaid intellectual property and in violation of Barron's copyright interest in the disc.
3. **Limited Warranty.** Disclaimer of implied warranties. If the disc fails to function in a satisfactory manner, Barron's sole liability to any purchaser or user shall be limited to refunding the price paid for same by said purchaser or user. Barron's makes no other warranties, express or implied, with respect to the disc. Barron's specifically disclaims any warranty of fitness for a particular purpose or of merchantability.
4. **Consequential Damages.** Barron's shall not be liable under any circumstances for indirect, incidental, special, or consequential damages resulting from the purchase or use of the disc.

The MP3 disc contains 15 tracks. Below is a list of track titles to make it easy for you to locate a specific topic of interest to you.

Track 1: Introduction

Track 2: Pronunciation

Track 3: Greetings/Exchanges

Track 4: Expressions/Commands

Track 5: Basic Vocabulary

Track 6: More Vocabulary

Track 7: Numbers/Plurality/Agreement

Track 8: Questions/Location/Time

Track 9: *Estar* and *Ser*

Track 10: Pronouns/Verbs/Tenses

Track 11: Irregular Verbs/More Tenses

Track 12: More Tenses/Prepositions

Track 13: Infinitive Constructions

Track 14: Subjunctive Mood

Track 15: Practice Tips/Review

© Copyright 2014 by William C. Harvey

All rights reserved.

No part of this publication may be reproduced or distributed in any form or by any means without the written permission of the copyright owner.

All inquiries should be addressed to:
Barron's Educational Series, Inc.
250 Wireless Boulevard
Hauppauge, New York 11788
www.barronseduc.com

Library of Congress Catalog Card No. 2013020056

ISBN: 978-1-4380-7409-2

Library of Congress Cataloging-in-Publication Data
Harvey, William C.
How to get an A+ in Spanish / William C. Harvey.
pages cm
Includes index.
ISBN 978-1-4380-7409-2
1. Spanish language—Study and teaching (Secondary). 2. Spanish language—Textbooks for foreign speakers—English. 3. Spanish language—Grammar. 4. Spanish language—Spoken Spanish. I. Title.
PC4065.H37 2014
468.2'421—dc23   2013020056

Printed in the United States of America
9 8 7 6 5 4 3 2 1

Contents

Chapter 1 The Sounds / 1

Chapter 1 reviews the pronunciation of both vowels and consonants, the alphabet, intonation, accentuation, and gives insights about breaking down words into separate syllables.

Chapter 2 Expressions / 15

In Chapter 2, students are taught what to listen for before responding intelligently to any normal salutation or courteous phrase. They are also given tips on how to utilize the "question words" in order to formulate a quick response or create questions by themselves.

Chapter 3 Vocabulary / 35

The basic vocabulary groups are introduced in Chapter 3, along with word lists not found in many Spanish textbooks. All terminology is broken into three main categories: those words that are easy to remember, those that are repeatedly used in everyday conversations, and those that students consider to be more difficult.

Chapter 4 Grammar—Part One / 69

Chapter 4 systematically teaches how the language is "built"—from the simplest concept to the more complex. Topics include the parts of speech, the sentence, the use of nouns with articles and descriptive adjectives.

Chapter 5   Grammar—Part Two / 97

Coverage of Spanish grammar continues in Chapter 5, with still more parts of speech, such as the demonstratives, possessives, pronouns, prepositions, and adverbs. Much like the previous chapter, the emphasis is on explaining how grammar works when words come together in a sentence.

Chapter 6   Verbs / 127

Spanish verbs are the focus of Chapter 6. All the basic verb tenses are explained through the use of shortcuts, and helpful practice activities are included on nearly every page.

Chapter 7   Tough Topics / 161

Chapter 7 confronts the classic problem areas for Spanish students by briefly explaining what they are and how to deal with them. These include using the subjunctive mood, reflexive verbs, verb infinitives, verbs like *gustar*, and the passive voice.

Chapter 8   Let's Review / 185

To review the learning of any language, it's best to break the process down into a variety of skill-based topics. Important practice suggestions are outlined here, as well as tips on how to maintain an A+ in Spanish.

Más Práctica / 207

End-of-book practice activities and exercises.

From the Author

How to Get an A+ in Spanish is specifically designed for those students who believe that learning Spanish is difficult, confusing, and sometimes overwhelming, but want to study it anyway. The book is also for those who have fallen behind in their Spanish course and need shortcuts to catch up with their lessons. The truth is, no matter where students are in the process of learning a new language, there is still hope. In fact, there is a way to get an A+ in Spanish.

As for those who are already doing well in Spanish and truly enjoying the experience, they have not been forgotten either. The tips and secrets to communication in this book are also designed to enhance what they know, accelerate their learning, and raise their skills to the next level regardless of where they are in the process. I believe that any English speaker who is trying to learn Spanish will benefit from the "inside information" provided in this guidebook. More important, this book can easily be used as a supplement to any other Spanish-learning program.

So, if you are looking for the key to become fluent in Spanish, read on. Everything you need to know is just ahead. Soon, if you pay close attention, you too will be able to understand, speak, read, and write in *español*. And, the great news is . . . it won't be as painful as you think!

Tu profesor,

Bill Harvey

How to Use This Guidebook

How to Get an A+ in Spanish is divided into eight unique chapters, each one discussing a different aspect of learning Spanish. Whenever you like, simply turn to the Table of Contents and select the topic you need. This book also provides you with specialized teaching segments, which are scattered throughout the text. All you do is watch for the special icon. But don't just skim over this material. Everything you read in this book is important and will help simplify your language lessons from class. Here are the icons to search for:

 ¡OYE!
(A quick helpful comment from the author)

 ¡PALABRAS EXTRAS!
(Additional Spanish words that students need to know)

 ¡CONVERSEMOS!
(Suggestions on how to improve your conversational Spanish skills)

 ¡LEE Y ESCRIBE!
(Secrets to improve your reading and writing in Spanish)

 ¿QUIERES PRACTICAR?
(Short practice exercises and review activities)

 ¡SECRETOS!
(Cultural insights that make learning Spanish more fun)

GETTING STARTED

Much like learning any new subject or skill, certain steps must be followed in order to have success. Things you'll need to consider include finding the best study environment, evaluating your instructor and course materials, overcoming your fears about learning Spanish, and determining how much time, money, and effort you intend to invest in the process. It might also be wise to keep track of everything you learn along the way. These steps are extremely important, so take time to think them through before turning to Chapter 1.

Chapter 1
Capítulo Uno

The Sounds
Los Sonidos

THE VOWELS

As you practice speaking Spanish, remember that the vowel sounds—*A, E, I, O, U*—are the secret to being understood in the language. This English pronunciation guide will help to get you started:

a (ah, like **"Father"**) *la, ta, sa, pa, fa*

e (eh, like **"let"**) *pe, fe, le, se, be*

i or *y** (ee, like **"Tina"**) *mi, pi, bi, ni, fi*

o (oh, like **"clone"**) *cho, to, mo, bo, lo*

u** (oo, like **"tulips"**) *tu, mu, su, pu, fu*

Look! Put the five words from above together, and you can practice the Spanish vowel sounds:

Father let Tina clone tulips.

a e i o u

Obviously, the best way to practice the vowels *(las vocales)* is to listen to a native speaker and then repeat what you hear. Fortunately, most Spanish programs include these kinds of audio exercises. The great news about Spanish is that the vowels are pronounced the same way almost every time. Once you've learned them, you won't have to worry about the subject again.

¡CONVERSEMOS!

Before you begin speaking Spanish, don't forget these three important tips on how to pronounce your sounds correctly:

1. First, avoid gliding or "stretching out" the sounds like we do in English. In other words, *"Acapulco"* is pronounced "ah-kah-pool-koh," not "ahhh-kahhh-poool-kohhh."

2. Second, remember that Spanish words have little or no "aspiration" (expelling puffs of air) when you pronounce them. This may require practice so try reading the vowels and syllables again, but this time without much aspiration.

3. Third, bear in mind that Spanish sounds are usually made toward the front of the mouth instead of way in the back.

---

*The letter *y* means "and," and is pronounced exactly like an *i*.

**The *u* sound changes when it becomes part of *que* or *qui* (i.e., *quesadilla*) and *gue* or *gui* (i.e., *guitarra*).

DIPHTHONGS

Two vowels can merge to form something called a "diphthong" (dif-thong). Diphthongs (*los diptongo*s) combine weak vowels (*u, i*) or *y* with strong vowels (*a, e, o*) to form a blended new sound. Bear in mind that you can blend two "weak" vowels together, but never two "strong" ones! To remember this rule, just memorize these two little jingles:

You (*u*) and **I** (*i*) are **weak**!
When **two** are **strong**, there's **no diphthong**!

Here's a typical list of Spanish diphthongs. Practice the "blending" of each pair of letters:

DIPHTHONG	PRONUNCIATION	EXAMPLE
ai or *ay*	<u>ai</u>sle	*aire* (air)
au	h<u>ou</u>se	*aula* (room)
ei or *ey*	th<u>ey</u>	*ley* (law)
eu	wa<u>yw</u>ard	*Europa* (Europe)
ia	<u>ya</u>rd	*enviar* (to send)
ie	<u>ye</u>s	*tienda* (store)
io	<u>yo</u>re	*apio* (celery)
iu	<u>you</u>	*viuda* (widow)
oi or *oy*	t<u>oy</u>	*doy* (I give)
ua	<u>wa</u>nt	*guante* (glove)
ue	<u>way</u>	*muestra* (sample)
ui or *uy*	<u>wee</u>k	*muy* (very)
uo	<u>wo</u>ke	*cuota* (dues)

A "triphthong" (*el triptongo*) is a blending of three vowels into a single syllable, specifically one strong vowel in between two weak vowels. Stretch the muscles in your mouth as you read aloud:

TRIPHTHONG	PRONUNCIATION	EXAMPLE
iai	yipe	*cambiáis* (you change)
iei	yea	*enviéis* (that you send)
uai or *uay*	wise	*Paraguay*
uei or *uey*	wait	*buey* (ox)

¿Quieres Practicar?

a.) Say each vowel clearly before looking up their translations:

el pan	*el coco*	*la espinaca*	*la uva*
la pera	*el tomate*	*la lechuga*	*el encurtido*

b.) Which of these combinations are *not* diphthongs?

cuadra	*maestro*	*criada*	*leemos*	*viudo*
abuela	*nieve*	*afeite*	*causa*	*real*

THE CONSONANTS: *C, D, G, H, J, LL, Ñ, Q, R, RR, V, Z*

The Spanish consonants make different sounds, too. They are produced by blocking the air partially or completely in speech. Since Spanish is "phonetic," most of these sounds are pronounced the way they are written:

SPANISH LETTER	ENGLISH SOUND
c (after an *e* or *i*)	s as in Sam (*cigarro*)
ch	ch as in China (*chica*)
d (between vowels, final)	th as in that (*nada, verdad*)
g (after an *e* or *i*)	h as in Harry (*general*)
h	silent, like the k in knife (*hola*)
j	h as in hot (*Juan*)
ll	y as in yes (*llama*)
ñ	ny as in canyon (*niño*)
q (followed by *ue* or *ui*)	k as in kit (*tequila*)
r (beginning, after *l, n*)	"rolled" r (*Rosa, río*)
rr	"rolled" r (*carro*)
v	b as in blue (*Victor*)
z	s as in sun (*cerveza*)

The letters *b, f, k, l, m, n, p, s, t* and *y* are somewhat similar to their English equivalents and don't need to be studied. The same holds true for Spanish words that begin with *w* or *x*, only because there aren't that many of them.

These are the only consonants that you'll need to work on—*c, d, g, h, j, ll, ñ, q, r, rr, v, z*—and these five tips will help you learn them faster:

THE FIVE STEPS

1. *z, h, j, v* (*z* = s, *h* is silent, *j* = h, *v* = b)
2. *c, g* (*c* = s, *g* = h after *e, i*)
3. *q* (*qu* = k)
4. *d, r* (like English, except when they fall between vowels or are the final letter *d* = "th" in "that" and "*r*" = "dd" in "wedding")
5. *ll, ñ, rr* (*ll* = y, *ñ* = ny, *rr* = "purring" sound, where tongue flaps against the roof of the mouth)

Now use the five clues to pronounce these consonants correctly:

   Cecilia, general, hueso, julio, lleno, nada, niño, quiere, parar, terror, vino, zapato

Many online educational websites include both vowels and consonant drills, with audio tools so web users can listen to the correct pronunciation of words. As you practice aloud, notice that most Spanish consonants are softer than their English equivalents, with the exception of the stronger *r* and *rr* sounds.

¡CONVERSEMOS!

Here's how some learners have eventually developed the ability to roll their "r's": Bend the tip of your tongue up very slightly just behind your top gums. Specifically, the tip of your tongue should be loose and just below the roof of the mouth between the upper teeth and the hard palate. Tense your tongue, but leave the tip loose to vibrate. Breathe out, allowing your tongue to vibrate with the passing air. This should produce somewhat of a "purring" sound. The rolling "r" sound is just the flutter of a tongue with the passing air, not a special curl or a fold.

¿Quieres Practicar?

Pronounce these common words. Remember to sound out each letter:

amigo	*granja*	*plaza*
amor	*guerrero*	*pollo*
carro	*hombro*	*quince*
español	*macho*	*reina*
experiencia	*mujer*	*señor*

¡LEE Y ESCRIBE!

The Spanish dieresis (*ü*) is used to obtain a "w" sound in front of certain vowels. For example, *güe* and *güi* are pronounced gwe and gwi, such as *pingüino* (penguin).

ACCENTUATION: *A-E-I-O-U-N-S*

Accentuation or "stress" refers to the loudness on a part of a word. In Spanish, one part of a word is usually stressed louder than the others. Stress is important because it can completely change the meaning of a word. Read these aloud: *papá* (father); *papa* (potato).

The rules for stress or accentuation in Spanish are particularly important when you are trying to pronounce a written word. For example, parts of words with vowels that have an accent mark (*á, é, í, ó, ú*) are pronounced louder and with more emphasis (*o lé*). Here are the three main rules:

THE THREE RULES

  I. If there's no accent mark, the last part of the word is pronounced louder (*es pa <u>ñol</u>*).
 II. For words ending in a vowel *a, e, i, o, u* or *n* or *s*, the next to the last part of the word is stressed (*im por <u>tan</u> te*).
III. A written accent mark either denotes an exception to the rules above or a need to distinguish words that are similar in spelling but different in meaning:

    A. *in te rés* ends in *s*, so it normally should be stressed on the second to last syllable; an accent indicates that it is an exception.
    B. *dé* is the command "give"; without an accent, it is the preposition *de*, which means "of" or "from."

Leaving off the accent mark on a word is a spelling mistake, and may even cause confusion, so it's important to learn what it's there for. Also remember that for most Spanish words there are no accent marks, and the stress falls on the last syllable.

¡OYE!

Accent marks (acute accents) are frequently found on verb endings, question words, and demonstratives:

verb endings: *volvió, preparándome, tráiganos*
question words: *¿Qué?, ¿Cuánto?, ¿Cómo?*
demonstratives: *ése, aquél, ésto*

And here's a list of common Spanish words that have accent marks. Take a mental picture as you practice pronouncing each one:

sí (yes)
más (more)
música (music)
alegría (happiness, joy)
limón (lemon)
azúcar (sugar)
bebé (baby)
fútbol (soccer)
corazón (heart)

jardín (garden)
río (river)
médico (doctor)
sábado (Saturday)
canción (song)
periódico (newspaper)
campeón (champion)
fantástico (fantastic)
número (number)

 ¿Quieres Practicar?

Add an accent *only* to those words that require one. This will take some work:

1. *soledad* _____
2. *averiguais* _____
3. *violin* _____
4. *diecisiete* _____
5. *aula* _____
6. *ruido* _____
7. *tunel* _____
8. *examen* _____

9. *frances* _____
10. *murcielago* _____
11. *caracter* _____
12. *buey* _____
13. *capitulo* _____
14. *dame* _____
15. *vivi* _____

2. *averiguáis*   3. *violín*   7. *túnel*   9. *francés*   10. *murciélago*   11. *carácter*   13. *capítulo*   15. *viví*

INTONATION

"Intonation" refers to pitch, or the rising ↑ and falling ↓ of one's voice. In Spanish, normal statements end in a falling pitch (i.e., *Juan es mi amigo.* ↓). Questions that elicit information also end in a falling pitch, but they are never confused with statements because they always begin with question words (i.e., *¿Cómo se llama?* ↓). However, when a question elicits an answer that is a choice between two or more alternatives, the pitch rises with each choice, and then falls with the final option (*¿Quieres agua* ↑ *o leche?* ↓).

LINKING

In spoken Spanish, it is very common for sounds of words to "link," blend, or run together, especially when a word ends in the same letter that begins the next word. For example, *helado* (ice cream) and *el lado* (the side) are pronounced identically. When a word that ends in a vowel is followed by a word that begins with a vowel, those vowels are also linked into one syllable, even if they are different. For instance, *Puede ordenar* (He can order), sounds like one long word. Another example of linking occurs when a word that ends in a consonant is followed by a word that begins with a vowel. The final consonant is linked with the initial vowel sound, such as in the sentence, *Vamos al océano.* (Let's go to the ocean.), which also sounds like one long word.

 ¿Quieres Practicar?

Read these sentences as fast as you can, using the correct intonation. Then, translate them. Remember that information questions like these usually end in a falling pitch:

1. *¿Cómo se llama usted?*

2. *¿Dónde está el baño?*

3. *¿Quién es su amigo?*

4. *¿Cuánto cuesta este libro?*

5. *¿Cuántos años tiene usted?*

6. *¿Cómo está su familia?*

7. *¿Cuándo estudia español usted?*

8. *¿Cuál es su dirección?*

1. What's your name?
2. Where's the bathroom?
3. Who is your friend?
4. How much is this book?
5. How old are you?
6. How is your family?
7. When do you study Spanish?
8. What's your address?

SYLLABLES

You cannot be understood if you're not saying words correctly—in syllables. A syllable (*sílaba*) is a piece of a word that must contain at least one vowel, such as the three syllables in *Fran-cis-co*. To divide Spanish words into syllables, here are the rules:

THE TOP EIGHT

1. A single consonant (including *ch*, *ll*, and *rr*) is pronounced with the following break in syllables: *ca-be-za, mu-cha-cho, ce-bo-lla, gue-rra*.

2. Combinations of two consonants between vowels are generally separated: *car-ta, cin-co, tar-de*.

3. However, the combination is usually inseparable if the second consonant is *l* or *r*: *ta-bla, li-bro, pue-blo*.

4. When three or more consonants are together between vowels, generally the last one joins the next vowel (unless it is *l* or *r*): *ins-ti-gar, cons-tan-te, in-glés*.

5. Diphthongs and triphthongs form no separate syllables: *i-gual, ca-yen-do, oi-go, Pa-ra-guay, con-ti-nuéis*.

6. When two strong vowels are together in a word, they are separated into syllables: *cre-er, em-ple-an, le-o*.

7. There is also separation when there is an accented weak vowel before or after a strong vowel: *co-mí-an, grú-a, tí-a*.

8. The letter *y* is considered a consonant when a vowel follows it, and it remains with that vowel when the word is divided: *a-yu-da-mos, a-yu-na, a-yer*.

Do not spend too much time memorizing these rules on syllabication! For now, get a general idea of how to do it correctly, and then practice by speaking, reading, and writing in Spanish—one syllable at a time.

> **¡LEE Y ESCRIBE!**
>
> A tilde is a diacritical mark (an accent) that is placed over a letter to change its pronunciation. In Spanish, it is used over the letter *n* to indicate an "ny" sound, as in *mañana*. It is important to be able to pronounce this sound to speak Spanish correctly.

¿Quieres Practicar?

Read these words aloud correctly by dividing them into syllables:

1. *milla*
2. *extraño*
3. *tío*
4. *escribir*
5. *construcción*
6. *enviáis*
7. *Uruguay*
8. *carro*
9. *miércoles*
10. *pagaréis*

> Feeling overwhelmed? Don't be. Spanish can't be conquered in a day!

THE ALPHABET

Take a few moments to review the alphabet (*el abecedario*) in Spanish. You may have learned the sounds the letters make, but to get an A+ you'll need the names for the letters themselves:

a (ah)	*h* (ah'-cheh)	*ñ* (ehn'-yeh)*	*u* (oo)
b (beh)	*i* (ee)	*o* (oh)	*v* (veh)
c (seh)	*j* (hoh'-tah)	*p* (peh)	*w* (doh'-bleh veh)
ch (cheh)*	*k* (kah)	*q* (koo)	*x* (eh'-kees)
d (deh)	*l* (eh'-leh)	*r* (eh'-reh)	*y* (ee-gree-eh'-gah)
e (eh)	*ll* (eh'-yeh)*	*rr* (eh'-rreh)	*z* (seh'-tah)
f (eh'-feh)	*m* (eh'-meh)	*s* (eh'-seh)	
g (heh)	*n* (eh'-neh)	*t* (teh)	

Can you say the alphabet in Spanish—without looking?

¡OYE!

Unfortunately, although you can tell how a Spanish word is pronounced by its spelling, the reverse isn't always so. In fact, native Spanish speakers are often poor spellers. That's because Spanish is full of "homophones," words that are spelled differently but pronounced alike.

SPELLING

Spanish utilizes many of the same punctuation marks as English (period, comma, semicolon, etc.). However, when writing exclamations or questions in Spanish, you must include an upside-down mark at the beginning: *¿Cómo está? ¡Adiós!*

---

* According to the Royal Spanish Academy, these three letters have been removed from the "official" Spanish alphabet. However, people still refer to them when spelling out a word. Also remember that Spanish dialects do vary, so some textbooks will provide different pronunciation guides from the ones listed above.

There are also some differences in the use of capital letters (*las mayúsculas*) in Spanish. These are the rules:

THE BIG SIX

1. The first word of a sentence is always capitalized:
   ¿Cómo está?
2. Proper names of people, places, and things are capitalized:
   Carlos es de Cuba.
3. Days of the week and months of the year are not capitalized:
   lunes, el diez de mayo
4. Religions, nationalities, and languages are not capitalized:
   inglés y español
5. In titles of books or works of art, only the first word is capitalized:
   La casa de los espíritus
6. Most abbreviations are capitalized:
   E.E.U.U. (U.S.A.), Sr., Sra., Srta., Dr., Dra., etc.

¡CONVERSEMOS!

One reason many students choose to learn Spanish as a foreign language is because they've heard that it's easy to pronounce. Indeed that's the case—even though some of the sounds can be a little tough for foreigners to master. This relative ease in pronunciation stems from the phonetic nature of Spanish: by knowing the spelling of a word, you can almost always know how it's pronounced. The major exceptions are words of foreign origin, and in that case you have a head start if you know English, because most of them—words such as *marketing, hockey,* and *Internet* (yes, those are Spanish words)—come from English.

In reality, students of Spanish will commit spelling errors, and these are the main reasons why:

STUDENT SPELLING ERRORS

1. They apply English spelling patterns to Spanish words, such as inserting a double consonant, like "tt"or "ss" or deleting the letter "h."
2. They spell out a word as they pronounce it, which is dangerous if one cannot say the five Spanish vowels correctly.
3. They forget the unique Spanish markings such as *¿, ñ,* or *á.*
4. They don't know which words are capitalized in Spanish.
5. They seldom listen to, speak, read, or even study Spanish material, so writing the language becomes a very difficult task!

DIALECTS: SPAIN AND LATIN AMERICA

Spanish pronunciation is fairly straightforward, because there are regular rules for the pronunciation of each letter and letter combination, with very few exceptions. More important, most letters in Spanish represent a single sound. The pronunciation of some letters depends on the location of the letter in the word and the letters beside it. This is true for Spanish regardless of the country where it is spoken.

However, in the case of a few Spanish sounds, there are some minor differences. For example, the primary difference that most students will notice regarding pronunciation in Spain as compared to Latin America is the pronunciation of the letter *z*, which in Latin America is pronounced like the letter *s*, but in Spain can be pronounced like "th" in the word "think." This change occurs for both *z* and *c* before the letters *i* and *e*. In Spain, for example, *lápices* (pencils) is pronounced "láh-pee-thehs."

Here are some more differences in sound-making:

- In Argentina, the Spanish *ll* and *y* are pronounced more like the sound at the beginning of the word "jump."
- In other parts of Latin America and Spain, the *x* is pronounced as a "sh" or "th" sound, instead of its usual pronunciation.
- In Cuba, the final consonant letter on many words is often dropped entirely, so what you may hear is nothing but a steady stream of vowels sounds.

Nevertheless, despite such differences, they seldom block communication, so speakers of Spanish around the world can still easily understand one another. Also be aware that Spanish will sometimes be referred to as *castellano* instead of *español*. In certain contexts, *castellano* refers to the Spanish language as spoken in Spain and various metropolitan regions of the world, while *español* is a more generic term, oftentimes referring to the language of Latin America.

¡SECRETOS!

Without a doubt, the best way to improve your pronunciation is to listen to others speaking Spanish correctly. You'll also learn a lot about Hispanic culture. By watching a Spanish movie, listening to Spanish music, or even overhearing a lengthy conversation in Spanish—on a regular basis—your pronunciation, comprehension, and cross-cultural skills will progress dramatically.

¡OYE!

Some learners struggle with Spanish pronunciation for personal reasons. For example, foreign-born students often have trouble in Spanish class when instructions are in English, since English may be their second or third language. Others may struggle because they are physically or mentally challenged in a way that directly affects the language learning process. Nevertheless, studies prove that new language skills can be acquired by just about anyone!

¿Quieres Practicar?

How fast can you say these tongue twisters—without hurting yourself?

1. *Tres tristes tigres trillaron trigo en un trigal.*

2. *Compre poco capa parda, porque el que poco capa parda compra poco capa parda paga.*

3. *Ñoño Yáñez come ñame en las mañanas con el niño.*

3. Squeamish Yáñez eats yams in the mornings with the child.
2. Buy only a little brown cape, for he who buys only a little brown cape pays only for a little brown cape.
1. Three sad tigers threshed wheat in a wheat field.

HOW TO GET AN A+

Go back and read through this chapter about Spanish pronunciation again, noting anything that you didn't quite understand the first time. Research the topic online, review it with your instructor, or study it with a fellow student or friend. If you don't learn about the sounds of Spanish now, it will probably create a problem for you later. Besides, how can we delve into the next chapter—which teaches Spanish expressions—if you can't even pronounce a word correctly? Start working on your speaking skills today!

Chapter 2
Capítulo Dos

Expressions
Expresiones

BASIC CONVERSATION

The following are called "survival expressions" in Spanish-speaking countries, and must be memorized immediately. Practice saying them in front of a mirror:

Hi.	*Hola.*
Good morning.	*Buenas días.*
Good afternoon.	*Buenas tardes.*
Good evening or Good night.	*Buenas noches.*
How are you?	*¿Cómo está usted?* (formal relationship)
	¿Cómo estás tú? (informal relationship)
How's it going?	*¡Qué tal!*
Fine, thanks.	*Bien, gracias.*
Not bad.	*Regular.*
Very well.	*Muy bien.*
What's happening?	*¿Qué pasa?*
Nothing much.	*Sin novedad.*
And you?	*¿Y usted?* (formal)
	¿Y tú? (informal)
Good-bye.	*Adiós.*

¡CONVERSEMOS!

Buenos días is used until about noon, *Buenas tardes* is used from about noon until dark, and *Buenas noches* is used to express both "Good evening" and "Good night." *Hola* can be used to greet others at any time of day.

Continue to chatter away using complete memorized expressions, most of which are found in classic textbook dialogs. Let's divide them into practical topics:

COMMON COURTESIES

Please.	*Por favor.*
Thanks.	*Gracias.*
Thank you very much.	*Muchas gracias.*
That's so kind of you.	*Muy amable.*
You're welcome.	*De nada.*
Just a moment.	*Un momento.*
Excuse me.	*Con permiso.*
Pardon me.	*Perdón.*
May I come in?	*¿Se puede entrar?*

Go ahead.	*Pase.*
Come in.	*Adelante.*
Is that taken?	*¿Está ocupado/a?*
Bless you!	*¡Salud!*

¡PALABRAS EXTRAS!

Several expressions in Spanish have synonyms; that is, there are other expressions which carry their same meaning, depending upon the local usage. Here is one example:

Excuse me   *Con permiso/Perdone/Disculpe*

MEETING SOMEONE

What's your name?	*¿Cómo se llama usted?* (formal)
	¿Cómo te llamas? (informal)
My name is . . .	*Me llamo . . .*
I want to introduce you to . . .	*Quiero presentarle a . . .*
Delighted to meet you.	*Encantado/a de conocerle.*
The pleasure is mine.	*El gusto es mío.*
Nice to meet you.	*Mucho gusto.*
Same to you.	*Igualmente.*

¡SECRETOS!

Notice how Spanish has both a formal and an informal (or "familiar") way to talk to another person. Informal Spanish is used with family members, close friends, or children. See how the pronouns and verbs change whenever that happens, but don't fret, we will discuss this more in detail just ahead.

GOOD TIDINGS

Welcome!	*¡Bienvenido!*
Congratulations!	*¡Felicitaciones!*
Happy anniversary!	*¡Feliz aniversario!*
Happy birthday!	*¡Feliz cumpleaños!*
Merry Christmas!	*¡Feliz navidad!*
Happy New Year!	*¡Próspero año nuevo!*
Happy holidays!	*¡Felices fiestas!*

¡OYE!

People often call out to one another in nothing more than short, friendly expressions. Remember that some one-liners do not directly translate into English:

See you soon!   *¡Hasta la vista!*   Take it easy!   *¡Qué le vaya bien!*

FAREWELL EXCHANGES

We'll see you!	*¡Nos vemos!*
See you later!	*¡Hasta luego!*
See you soon!	*¡Hasta la vista!*
See you tomorrow!	*¡Hasta mañana!*
Good luck!	*¡Buena suerte!*
Have a nice trip!	*¡Buen viaje!*
Give my regards to . . .!	*¡Me saluda a . . .!*
Have a nice day!	*¡Qué tenga buen día!*
Take it easy!	*¡Qué le vaya bien!*
Get well!	*¡Qué se mejore!*
Go with God!	*¡Qué vaya con Dios!*
Have a good time!	*¡Qué disfrute!*

¡PALABRAS EXTRAS!

The word *Qué* is part of countless expressions in Spanish. Pick one you like and try it out today:

What a shame!	*¡Qué lástima!*	So what!	*¡Qué importa!*
How sad!	*¡Qué triste!*	What a joke!	*¡Qué chiste!*
What a pity!	*¡Qué pena!*	How funny!	*¡Qué chistoso!*

PERSONAL HEALTH

How are you feeling?	*¿Cómo se siente?*
I'm hungry.	*Tengo hambre.*
I'm thirsty.	*Tengo sed.*
I'm hot.	*Tengo calor.*
I'm cold.	*Tengo frío.*
I'm sleepy.	*Tengo sueño.*
I'm happy.	*Estoy feliz.*
I'm sad.	*Estoy triste.*
I'm worried.	*Estoy preocupado.* (male)
	Estoy preocupada. (female)
I'm tired.	*Estoy cansado.* (male)
	Estoy cansada. (female)
I'm sick.	*Estoy enfermo.* (male)
	Estoy enferma. (female)

¡OYE!

In Spanish grammar, the last letter of most descriptive words ends in either an *o* (which refers to males) or an *a* (which refers to females). This is called "gender" and will be explained in the next chapter.

¿Quieres Practicar?

React to these expressions as quickly as you can:

1. *Hola. ¿Cómo está usted?* _____
2. *Gracias, muy amable.* _____
3. *¿Qué pasa?* _____
4. *Mucho gusto.* _____
5. *¡Hasta luego!* _____
6. *¡Felicitaciones!* _____
7. *¿Cómo se llama usted?* _____
8. *¡Felices fiestas!* _____

¡SECRETOS!

Spanish is full of expressions that make references to God (*Dios*). These are the most common ones:

God willing!	*¡Si Dios quiera!*
Oh my gosh!	*¡Dios mío!*
Go with God!	*¡Vaya con Dios!*
Thank goodness!	*¡Gracias a Dios!*
Good God!	*¡Válgame Dios!*

QUICK COMMENTS

Stay in the conversational loop. Interject one of the following, which simply expresses that you understand what's going on:

I agree!	*¡De acuerdo!*
I hope so!	*¡Ojalá!*
I think so!	*¡Creo que sí!*
I see!	*¡Ya veo!*
I'm so glad!	*¡Me alegro!*
Me, too!	*¡Yo también!*
Not me!	*¡Yo no!*
That's for sure!	*¡Es cierto!*
That's great!	*¡Qué bueno!*

> I know it seems like you've bitten off more than you can chew, but just remember that joke about eating an *elefante*: it can be done . . . but one bite at a time!

Expressions work wonders in a classroom setting, because they send a message to everyone that you're aware of what the teacher is talking about. Write down your favorites today:

You're right!	*¡Tiene razón!*
You're kidding!	*¡No me diga!*
Whatever you want!	*¡Lo que quiera!*

Of course!	*¡Por supuesto!*
Sure!	*¡Claro!*
Maybe!	*¡Quizás!*
No problem!	*¡No hay problema!*
No wonder!	*¡Con razón!*
It doesn't matter!	*¡No importa!*
Really?	*¿Es verdad?*
Isn't that right?	*¿No es cierto?*
Are you sure?	*¿Está seguro/a?*

¿Quieres Practicar?

How would you say these expressions *en español*?

1. I hope so! _____

2. Me, too! _____

3. That's for sure! _____

4. You're kidding! _____

5. Maybe! _____

6. It doesn't matter! _____

7. Really? _____

1. *¡Ojalá!*
2. *¡Yo, también!*
3. *¡Es cierto!*
4. *¡No me diga!*
5. *¡Quizás!*
6. *¡No importa!*
7. *¿Es verdad?*

¡OYE!

Restrooms in Latin America will have these words written on their doors:

Ladies *Damas*   Gentlemen *Caballeros*

WHAT TO SAY WHEN YOU GET STUCK

Be aware that everything from now on will be presented in the "formal" style of speech, which refers to the individual "you" as *usted* (abbreviated *Ud.*). The word itself is not required in every sentence. Here's what you say when you get stuck:

What?	*¿Qué?*
How's that?	*¿Cómo?*
Again, please.	*Otra vez, por favor.*
I'm sorry.	*Lo siento.*
I speak very little.	*Hablo muy poquito.*
Do you speak English?	*¿Habla Ud. inglés?*
I'm learning Spanish.	*Estoy aprendiendo español.*
Could you repeat that?	*¿Podría repetirlo?*
Please speak more slowly.	*Favor de hablar más despacio.*
How do you say . . . in Spanish?	*¿Cómo se dice . . . en español?*
Do you understand?	*¿Entiende Ud.?*
I don't know much Spanish.	*No sé mucho español.*
I don't speak Spanish.	*No hablo español.*
I don't comprehend.	*No comprendo.*
I don't understand.	*No entiendo.*
I don't remember.	*No recuerdo.*
What does that mean?	*¿Qué significa eso?*
Can you translate it?	*¿Puede traducirla?*
How do you write it?	*¿Cómo se escribe?*
How do you spell it?	*¿Cómo se deletrea?*
Letter by letter.	*Letra por letra.*
Word for word.	*Palabra por palabra.*

The phrases above will help clarify a message, get you out of difficulty, and send the signal that you're not giving up. That's the true mark of someone with an A+ in Spanish!

 ¡CONVERSEMOS!

Spanish has a variety of something called interjections, which are merely exclamatory outbursts that are expressed depending upon the scenario. Interjections sometimes differ from one region to the next:

Hush!	*¡Chitón!*	Cheers!	*¡Salud!*
Fiddlesticks!	*¡Pamplinas!*	Wow!	*¡Caramba!*
Ouch!	*¡Ay!*		

¿Quieres Practicar?

Write the English below each phrase and then practice the exchange:

1. *¿Entiende Ud.?*

_____

2. *No, no entiendo. Favor de hablar más despacio.*

_____

3. *¿Podría repetirlo?*

_____

4. *¿Cómo se deletrea la palabra? Letra por letra, por favor.*

_____

1. Do you understand?
2. No, I don't understand. Please speak more slowly.
3. Would you repeat it?
4. How do you spell the word? Letter by letter, please.

TEACHER'S TALK

There are some Spanish expressions that you hear regularly in the language classroom. Although you may not understand everything, pay attention to any comments that your teacher uses daily:

Ready?	*¿Listos?*
Now . . .	*Ahora . . .*
Let's . . .	*Vamos a . . .*
Like this.	*Así.*
Any questions?	*¿Hay preguntas?*
You can begin.	*Pueden comenzar.*
All done?	*¿Ya terminaron?*
Excellent.	*Excelente.*
Fine.	*Bien.*
Okay.	*Bueno.*
Fantastic.	*Fantástico.*
Great.	*Muy bien.*
Good job.	*Bien hecho.*

This is what I want.	*Esto es lo que quiero.*
This way.	*De esta manera.*
That's it.	*Eso es.*
The next one.	*Lo que sigue.*
The previous one.	*El anterior.*
The last one.	*El último.*
The same thing.	*La misma cosa.*
The opposite.	*Lo contrario.*
The other one.	*El otro.*
Face to face.	*Cara a cara.*
Step by step.	*Paso a paso.*
Little by little.	*Poco a poco.*

¡PALABRAS EXTRAS!

The word *vez* also means "time," but notice how it's used differently:

una vez	once
dos veces	twice
muchas veces	many times

Here are the TOP TEN classroom instructions in Spanish:

1.	Quiet, please.	*Silencio, por favor.*
2.	Answer the question.	*Conteste la pregunta.*
3.	Raise your hand.	*Levante la mano.*
4.	Read it.	*Léalo.*
5.	Sit down.	*Siéntese.*
6.	Write it down.	*Escríbalo.*
7.	Open your book.	*Abra su libro.*
8.	Say it.	*Dígalo.*
9.	Repeat it.	*Repítalo.*
10.	Listen.	*Escuche.*

¡OYE!

No two Spanish teachers are exactly alike, so you will have to record some expressions on your own. For instance, one teaching technique is to ask lots of questions, so take note of those that your instructor uses all the time:

<u>What</u>'s this?	*¿<u>Qué</u> es esto?*
<u>How many</u> are there?	*¿<u>Cuántos</u> hay?*
<u>Whose</u> is this?	*¿<u>De quién</u> es esto?*

¿Quieres Practicar?

Connect each English word with the appropriate Spanish expression:

1. *Siéntese.* book
2. *Silencio, por favor.* pen
3. *Léalo.* question
4. *Conteste la pregunta.* noise
5. *Escríbalo.* chair

1. chair 2. noise 3. book 4. question 5. pen

¡PALABRAS EXTRAS!

Read up on the difference between formal and informal commands in Spanish. These are a few examples:

VERB	FORMAL	INFORMAL
LOOK: *mirar*	*Mire Ud.*	*Mira tú*
OPEN: *abrir*	*Abra Ud.*	*Abre tú*
COME: *venir*	*Venga Ud.*	*Ven tú*

COMMON QUESTIONS

Many of the first expressions you'll hear will actually be questions that request personal information. Some are longer, but still need to be studied as a single word or phrase:

What's your first name?	*¿Cuál es su primer nombre?*
What's your last name?	*¿Cuál es su apellido?*
Where are you from?	*¿De dónde es Ud.?*
Where do you live?	*¿Dónde vive Ud.?*
What's your address?	*¿Cuál es su dirección?*
What's your zip code?	*¿Cuál es su zona postal?*
What do you do?	*¿A qué se dedica Ud.?*
What grade are you in?	*¿En qué grado está?*
How old are you?	*¿Cuántos años tiene Ud.?*
What's your phone number?	*¿Cuál es su número de teléfono?*
What's your area code?	*¿Cuál es su código telefónico?*
What's your email address?	*¿Cuál es su correo electrónico?*

¡LEE Y ESCRIBE!

Consider creating a personal interview form so you can practice these simple questions. Many of the "interview" phrases begin with one of the following words, so learn how to write them ASAP!

Do you have . . .?	*¿Tiene . . .?*
Do you want . . .?	*¿Quiere . . .?*
Do you need . . .?	*¿Necesita . . .?*
Do you like . . .?	*¿Le gusta . . .?*

TIME AND WEATHER EXPRESSIONS

Successful Spanish students also exchange one-liners about the time, calendar, and weather:

What time is it?	*¿Qué hora es?*
It's (time) . . .	*Son las . . ./Es la . . .*
At what time?	*¿A qué hora?*
At (time) . . .	*A las . . ./A la . . .*

What's the date?	*¿Cuál es la fecha?*
It's (date) . . .	*Es el . . .*
When was it?	*¿Cuándo fue . . .?*
It was . . .	*Fue . . .*

right now	*ahora mismo*
for today	*para hoy*
every day	*todos los días*
for tomorrow	*para mañana*
over the weekend	*durante el fin de semana*
in the evening	*de la noche*
at midnight	*a la medianoche*
at noon	*al mediodía*
tonight	*esta noche*
last night	*anoche*
yesterday	*ayer*
next month	*el próximo mes*
last week	*la semana pasada*
this year	*este año*
an hour ago	*hace una hora*
the day after tomorrow	*pasado mañana*
the day before yesterday	*anteayer*
all the time	*todo el tiempo*
the morning (A.M.)	*de la mañana*
the afternoon, night (P.M.)	*de la tarde, noche*
in an hour	*en una hora*
in five minutes	*en cinco minutos*

How's the weather?	*¿Qué tiempo hace?*

It's cold.	*Hace frío.*
It's hot (heat).	*Hace calor.*
It's nice weather.	*Hace buen tiempo.*
It's sunny.	*Hace sol.*
It's windy.	*Hace viento.*
It's cloudy.	*Está nublado.*
It's raining.	*Está lloviendo.*
It's snowing.	*Está nevando.*
It's foggy.	*Hay niebla.*

¡CONVERSEMOS!

Spanish speakers add a lot of "tag questions" at the end of their sentences. These three are the most popular. Don't forget to raise your voice on the last part!

It's sunny, right?	Hace sol, ¿no?
	Hace sol, ¿no es cierto?
	Hace sol, ¿verdad?

¿Quieres Practicar?

Answer these questions aloud in either Spanish or English:

¿Qué hora es?

¿Cuántos años tiene usted?

¿Qué tiempo hace?

¿Cuál es su correo electrónico?

¿Cuál es su primer nombre?

¿Dónde vive usted?

¿Cuál es la fecha?

¿Cuál es su código telefónico?

TRANSITIONAL PHRASES

This next group contains transitional phrases that allow speakers to converse in Spanish more fluidly—just like an A+ student! Create sentences using words that you saw earlier:

Above all . . .	*Sobre todo . . .*	*Sobre todo, aprendo español.*
According to . . .	*Según . . .*	*Según el libro, ¡no hay problema!*
Although . . .	*Aunque . . .*	*Aunque tengo hambre, no tengo sed.*
At first . . .	*Al principio . . .*	*Al principio,*
At last . . .	*Por fin . . .*	
At least . . .	*Por lo menos . . .*	

Besides . . .	*Además . . .*	_____
But . . .	*Pero . . .*	_____
By the way . . .	*A propósito . . .*	_____
For example . . .	*Por ejemplo . . .*	_____
However . . .	*Sin embargo . . .*	_____
In general . . .	*En general . . .*	_____
In my opinion . . .	*En mi opinión . . .*	_____
In spite of . . .	*A pesar de . . .*	_____
Little by little . . .	*Poco a poco . . .*	_____
On the contrary . . .	*A lo contrario . . .*	_____
So . . .	*Así que . . .*	_____
Then . . .	*Entonces . . .*	_____
Therefore . . .	*Por eso . . .*	_____
Without a doubt . . .	*Sin duda . . .*	_____
Still/Yet . . .	*Todavía . . .*	_____

¡SECRETOS!

When Spanish speakers pause because they need time to think about what they're going to say next, some of the following words come out. Why don't you do the same thing? Use three or four fillers to break up your sentences:

Let's see . . .	*A ver . . .*
Uh . . .	*Este . . .*
Well . . .	*Pues . . .*
O.K. . . .	*Bueno . . .*
What I mean is...	*Es decir . . .*
In other words . . .	*O sea . . .*
So . . .	*Así que . . .*

EXPRESSIONS FOR SPECIFIC PURPOSES

Before you get started with your favorite word group, picture yourself in the following scenarios, ready to chatter away:

ON THE PHONE

Hello!	*¡Aló!*
This is _____.	*Este es _____.*
Who's calling?	*¿Quién llama?*
Please wait a moment.	*Espere un momento, por favor.*
Could I speak with ___?	*¿Puedo hablar con _____?*
He/She is not home.	*No está en casa.*
When will he/she return?	*¿Cuándo regresa?*
May I leave a message?	*¿Puedo dejar un mensaje?*
Could I take a message?	*¿Puedo tomar un mensaje?*
I'll call back later.	*Llamaré más tarde.*
Please call me at ____.	*Favor de llamarme al número ____.*
You have the wrong number.	*Tiene el número equivocado.*
What number are you calling?	*¿Qué número está llamando?*

DINING OUT

May I see the menu?	*¿Podría ver el menú?*
Where are the restrooms?	*¿Dónde están los baños?*
I would like to order . . .	*Quisiera ordenar . . .*
Bring the bill, please.	*Tráigame la cuenta por favor.*
How much does it cost?	*¿Cuánto cuesta?*
I would like . . .	*Me gustaría . . .*
Is there any . . .?	*¿Hay . . .?*
Can you recommend . . .?	*¿Puede recomendarme . . .?*

> If you're tired of reading this stuff, go take a break.
> Get refreshed and come back later when you feel more motivated.

GETTING LOST

Can you please help me?	*¿Me podría ayudar, por favor?*
I'm looking for . . .	*Estoy buscando . . .*
I can't find . . .	*No encuentro . . .*
Could you please tell me . . .?	*¿Podría decirme . . .?*
Show me on the map.	*Enséñeme en el mapa.*

LOVE AND DATING

How pretty!	*¡Qué bonita!*
How handsome!	*¡Qué guapo!*
How good-looking!	*¡Qué simpático/a!*
You look beautiful!	*¡Te ves muy hermosa!*
It's for you!	*¡Es para ti!*
I love it!	*¡Me encanta!*
Are you seeing anyone?	*¿Estás saliendo con alguien?*
Would you like to dance?	*¿Quieres bailar?*
Can you give me your phone number?	*¿Puedes darme tu número de teléfono?*
Do you want to go out tonight?	*¿Salimos esta noche?*
I really like you.	*Me caes muy bien.*

¡OYE!

There may be some other cultural differences you're unaware of, so it would be wise to do some research about Spanish or Latin American social practices before you seriously date a native Spanish speaker.

EMERGENCIES

Help!	*¡Socorro!*
Fire!	*¡Fuego!*
Thief!	*¡Ladrón!*
Be careful!	*¡Cuidado!*
Watch out!	*¡Ojo!*
Call 9-1-1!	*¡Llame al 9-1-1!*
Help me!	*¡Ayúdeme!*
I had an accident.	*Tuve un accidente.*
What's the matter?	*¿Qué pasó?*
Where does it hurt?	*¿Dónde le duele?*
Are you injured?	*¿Está lastimado/a?*
Are you sick?	*¿Está enfermo/a?*
Are you lost?	*¿Se perdió usted?*
It's broken.	*Está roto/a.*
I have a problem.	*Tengo un problema.*
It doesn't work.	*No funciona.*

¿Quieres Practicar?

Just for fun, say one thing in Spanish that would be appropriate in the following circumstances:

1. You sit down in a Mexican restaurant to have lunch and the waitress approaches.

2. You want to address a Spanish speaker who looks like he is in a lot of pain.

3. You are about to tell someone in Spanish that you are interested in him/her.

IDIOMS

An idiom is a phrase that is used in place of grammatically conventional speech, for example, "I'm taking Spanish" instead of, "I'm currently enrolled in a Spanish class." People frequently use "idioms" in Spanish, so it would be wise to pick up as many of them as possible:

IDIOM	TRANSLATION	SAMPLE SENTENCE
Acabar de	to have just	*Acabo de comer.*
Dar a luz	to give birth	*¿Cuándo da a luz María?*
Dar de comer	to feed	
Dar el pésame	to express condolence	
Dar las gracias	to thank	
Dar un paseo	to take a walk	
Dar un recado	to leave a message	*Déjame un mensaje.*
Darse cuenta	to realize	*¿Te das cuenta?*
Darse por vencido	to give up	
Darse prisa	to hurry	
Decir la verdad	to tell the truth	*Siempre decimos la verdad.*
Dejar caer	to drop	
Estar a punto de	to be on the verge of	
Estar de acuerdo	to agree	*No están de acuerdo.*
Estar de buen humor	to be in a good mood	
Estar mal	to be in bad shape	
Hacer un viaje	to take a trip	*¿Cuándo haces un viaje?*
Hacer una visita	to pay a visit	

Ir a pie	to go on foot	_____
Poner la mesa	to set the table	*Ella nunca pone la mesa.*
Salir bien	to succeed	_____
Tener en cuenta	to keep in mind	_____
Tener ganas	to desire	*Tengo ganas de bailar.*
Tener que hacer	to have to do something	_____
Tener que ver	to have to do with	_____
Valer la pena de	to be worthwhile	_____

And here are a few of my favorite idiomatic expressions—in both languages:

Me viene de molde.	It fits me like a glove.
De buenas a primeras.	Right off the bat.
Toca madera.	Knock on wood.
Venga lo que viniere.	Come what may.
Le falta a uno un tornillo.	He's got a screw loose.

¡SECRETOS!

Slang, cursing, and name-calling are also part of everyday language, but will not be presented in this guidebook. Such elements of colloquial Spanish are usually acquired through real-life exposure, and will vary based upon regional dialect, social environment, and personal taste.

¿Quieres Practicar?

Write *VERDAD* (true) if the translation is correct or *FALSO* (false) if it isn't:

1. *estar de acuerdo*   to agree   *VERDAD* _____
2. *tener ganas*   to be hungry   _____
3. *ir a pie*   to go on foot   _____
4. *darse prisa*   to hurry   _____
5. *toca madera*   to be at fault   _____

5. *FALSO*
4. *VERDAD*
3. *VERDAD*
2. *FALSO*

HOW TO GET AN A+

Take a moment to review what we've learned so far about starting out in Spanish:

1. You need to commit 100% to the Spanish-learning process!
2. You must become familiar with the Spanish sound system as soon as possible!
3. You should begin speaking Spanish by trying out useful Spanish expressions!

Now it's time to learn more VOCABULARY in Spanish before saying anything else!

Chapter 3
Capítulo Tres

Vocabulary
El Vocabulario

Obviously, if you want to get an A+ in Spanish, you have to expand your vocabulary. But, instead of wasting time on worthless word drills and exercises, why not follow these three simple "steps" to learning Spanish more quickly:

Step One: Focus on words that are **SIMILAR** to English or are relatively easy to remember.

Step Two: Learn those words that are **REPEATED** time and again in daily conversation.

Step Three: List those words that are **DIFFICULT** to remember and practice them every day.

STEP ONE: FOCUS ON WORDS THAT ARE SIMILAR TO ENGLISH.

SPANISH WORDS THAT ARE ENGLISH WORDS

The group below is a list of Spanish loan words, since they were "borrowed" by English years ago. Instead of memorizing them, just read each one aloud, using a Spanish accent:

adobe	*pueblo*
bronco	*iguana*
burro	*loco*
cha-cha-cha	*machete*
chihuahua	*macho*
corral	*olé*
coyote	

 ## ¿Quieres Practicar?

Guess what's going on here!

1. *El bandido es un gringo.*

2. *La piñata es para mi fiesta.*

3. *El grupo de mariachis está en la hacienda.*

¡PALABRAS EXTRAS!

Notice how much Spanish is on a map of the United States!
Do you know their English translations?

Los Angeles	the angels
Santa Fe	holy faith
Rio Grande	big river
Florida	flowered
Montana	mountain

SPANISH WORDS THAT EVERYONE KNOWS

Plenty of Spanish words are well-known simply because they are used a lot. This is a list of vocabulary that many folks in the United States seem to know, even though they've never taken a Spanish class. Translate the ones you can understand:

adiós	good-bye
agua	water
americano	American
amigo	friend
amor	_____
bueno	_____
casa	_____
cerveza	_____
dinero	_____
español	_____
gracias	_____

¡CONVERSEMOS!

You have two kinds of vocabulary in Spanish, ACTIVE and PASSIVE:

1. Words you remember and use all the time. (ACTIVE)

2. Words you know but don't use all the time. (PASSIVE)

This is important, because if you are not speaking much Spanish right now, it doesn't mean necessarily that you don't know a lot of vocabulary.

> **¡SECRETOS!**
>
> "Spanglish" is a blend of both Spanish and English words, which occurs naturally when the two languages are spoken in the same geographical area (i.e., the Southwest) over an extended period of time. Use Spanglish vocabulary only if you have nowhere else to turn:
>
> | SPANISH | ENGLISH | SPANGLISH |
> |---------|---------|-----------|
> | *estacionar* | to park | *parquear* |
> | *la bicicleta* | bike | *la baika* |
> | *el almuerzo* | lunch | *el lonche* |

SPANISH WORDS THAT LOOK A LOT LIKE ENGLISH

Your textbook calls words like these "cognates" (Spanish and English words with the same origin). They're everywhere, and many share the same spelling and meaning:

OR-endings
actor
color
doctor

BLE-endings
admirable
terrible
favorable

AL-endings
animal
festival
general

AR-endings
similar
regular
popular

¿Quieres Practicar?

Although these patterns aren't true for every word in Spanish, chances are you'll be correct most of the time if you're guessing. There's no need to write the translation:

It is very popular.   *Es muy popular.*

It is very natural.   *Es _____.*

It is very terrible.   *Es _____.*

Here's the definition of a suffix (*el sufijo*) in Spanish. Look closely at the spelling of the words and you may be able to guess at what they mean:

EL SUFIJO
Una sílaba o letra que se añade al final de una
palabra para modificar su significado.

A syllable or letter that is added to the end of a
word in order to change its meaning.

They're not identical, but if you seek out the many similarities, the Spanish makes more sense!

SPANISH WORD ENDINGS

Learn these suffix patterns, and you might get that A+ a lot sooner than you think!

ENDINGS	SPANISH	ENGLISH
ico, ic	*romántico*	romantic
ente, ent	*diferente*	different
ción, tion	*construcción*	construction
oso, ous	*delicioso*	delicious
dad, ty	*electricidad*	electricity
rio, ry	*necesario*	necessary
ista, ist	*artista*	artist
sión, sion	*decisión*	decision
ismo, ism	*comunismo*	communism
mento, ment	*monumento*	monument
ía, y	*biografía*	biography
ama, am	*programa*	program

 ¡OYE!

Here's the process: Think about a word in English, change it's ending to Spanish, and now say it!

THINK: John is roman<u>tic</u>.　　　SAY: *Juan es román<u>tico</u>.*

THINK: The taco is deli<u>cious</u>.　　SAY: *El taco es deli<u>cioso</u>.*

For fun, read this sentence, and then guess how to say the two English words below in Spanish:

> *Hay un programa en la televisión sobre la biografía de Josef Stalin,*
> *el líder famoso de la revolución comunista en Rusia.*

Hay   *sobre*
There's   _____   about   _____

Can you translate the whole thing into English?

 **¡CONVERSEMOS!**

It's common in Spanish to add on the *ito* or *ita* endings when you'd like to indicate smallness or affection:

Mi abuel<u>ito</u> está en su cas<u>ita</u>.

My grandpa is in his little house.

Study these other word endings that make Spanish even easier to remember:

ENDINGS	SPANISH	ENGLISH
mente, ly	*probablemente*	probably
ema, em	*poema*	poem
cia, cy	*emergencia*	emergency
ivo, ive	*colectivo*	collective
culo, cle	*artículo*	article
cto, ct	*perfecto*	perfect
uro, ure	*futuro*	future
uto, ute	*bruto*	brute
ido, id	*ácido*	acid
ina, in	*vitamina*	vitamin
ina, ine	*medicina*	medicine

¿Quieres Practicar?

Translate this list as fast as you can. There's no reason to write anything:

1. *florista*   <u>florist</u>
2. *aniversario*
3. *comunidad*
4. *ambicioso*
5. *atención*

6. *inteligente*
7. *Atlántico*
8. *geografía*
9. *válido*
10. *nativo*

¡LEE Y ESCRIBE!

Suffixes are also used to give special meanings to words, which really helps when you're trying to understand what you're reading in Spanish. Make a copy of this list and use it as a guide!

ENDING	MEANING	EXAMPLE
-ada	similar to English suffix "-ful" or "-load"	*cuchara* (spoon); *cucharada* (spoonful)
-ado, -ido	similar to actions ending in "ed"	*pintar* (to paint); *pintado* (painted)
-ando/iendo	turns action words into "ing" words	*enseñar* (to teach); *enseñando* (teaching)
-anza	turns action words into things	*esperar* (to hope); *esperanza* (hope)
-ar, er, ir	basic verb endings	*hablar* (to speak); *comer* (to eat); *salir* (to leave)
-ario	indicates profession or place	*biblioteca* (library); *bibliotecario* (librarian)
-azo	a punch or hit of something	*bala* (bullet); *balazo* (gunshot or bullet wound)
-dor	person, place, or thing	*comer* (to eat); *comedor* (dining room)
-dura	indicates the effect of an action	*picar* (to pick at); *picadura* (insect bite)
-ería	place where items are made or sold	*zapato* (shoe); *zapatería* (shoe store)
-ero	variety of meanings	*sombra* (shade); *sombrero* (hat)—*vaca* (cow); *vaquero* (cowboy)
-és	indicates place of origin	Holanda (Holland); *holandés* (Dutch)
-eza	turns descriptions into things	*pura* (pure); *pureza* (purity)
-zaje	turns actions into things	*aprender* (to learn); *aprendizaje* (knowledge)

THE BEGINNING PART OF SPANISH WORDS

The prefix (*el prefijo*) is generally a short addition put at the beginning of a word. Guess at the meanings of these Spanish words without looking at the English:

BEGINNING	SPANISH	ENGLISH
anti- (against)	*antivirus*	antivirus
auto- (self)	*autodisciplina*	self-discipline
bi-, bis-, biz- (two)	*bilingüe*	bilingual
contra- (against)	*contrataque*	counterattack
des- (un-, undo, diminish)	*desafortunado*	unfortunate
homo- (same)	*homónimo*	homonym
inter- (between, among)	*interacción*	interaction
mono- (one)	*monótono*	monotonous
poli- (many)	*poligamia*	polygamy
pre- (before)	*predestinación*	predestination
semi- (medium, half)	*semifinalista*	semifinalist
sobre- (excessive, over)	*sobredosis*	overdose
super- (superior)	*superhombre*	superman
tele- (at a distance)	*telescopio*	telescope

Now, there's no need to panic if a Spanish word appears too complicated:

desafortunadamente

des	*afortunada*	*mente*
un	fortunate	ly

¡PALABRAS EXTRAS!

Healthcare Spanish is full of cognates. Many body parts, illnesses, and general medical words are very similar to English:

BODY PARTS	ILLNESSES	GENERAL
pelvis	*cáncer*	*hospital*
intestino	*influenza*	*farmacia*
arteria	*diabetes*	*operación*

FAKE SPANISH WORDS

Though most of the time you'll guess at word meanings correctly, there are a few fake or false cognates in Spanish, too. These could keep you from getting an A+ in Spanish!

SPANISH	ENGLISH MEANING
actual	present, of the present time
campo	countryside
collar	necklace
compromiso	promise
contestar	to answer
delito	crime
desgracia	misfortune
educado	well-mannered
embarazada	pregnant
éxito	success, outcome
largo	long
lectura	reading
molestar	to bother
pariente	relative
pretender	to try
realizar	to achieve
asistir	to attend
revolver	to stir, turn over
sensible	sensitive
suceso	event, happening
tormenta	storm

¿Quieres Practicar?

Careful as you translate! These sentences are not what they may seem:

1. *Robar collares es un delito.*

2. *Mi pariente está embarazada.*

3. *Juan es educado y sensible.*

1. Stealing necklaces is a crime.
2. My relative is pregnant.
3. Juan is well-behaved and sensitive.

¡OYE!

No doubt you're making lots of spelling errors as you write down Spanish words. Spelling only gets better over time. For tips on spelling, check out the shortcuts and tips in Chapter 2.

STEP TWO: LEARN THOSE WORDS THAT ARE REPEATED.

THE WORDS *EL* AND *LA*

El and *La* are called definite articles (*los artículos definidos*) and are the most common words in Spanish. They both mean "the," but are often linked to the topic of gender. The names for people, places, and things have gender in Spanish; that is, they are either masculine (m.) or feminine (f.). So, to distinguish them as a singular noun, you need to put either an *el* (m.) or a *la* (f.) in front of the word.

For example, *el niño* is "boy," while *la niña* is "girl." In a sentence, you can use *el* and *la* much like the word "the" in English: Look at the boy and the girl. (*Mire el niño y la niña.*) For plural nouns (more than one), change *el* to *los* and *la* to *las:* Look at the boys and the girls. (*Mire los niños y las niñas.*)

Although it sounds strange, the same masculine or feminine rule applies to objects and other nouns, too: telephone → *el teléfono*; computer → *la computadora*. Look at the telephones and the computers. (*Mire los teléfonos y las computadoras.*)

 ¡CONVERSEMOS!

If the noun ends in the letter *o* there's usually an *el* in front (i.e., *el cuarto, el muchacho*). Conversely, if the noun ends in an *a* there's a *la* in front (i.e., *la mesa, la doctora*). Of course, there are a few exceptions to the *el–la* rule (i.e., *el programa, el agua, la mano, el sofá, el problema*), so you'll have to remember them. Words not ending in either an *o* or *a* also need to be memorized (i.e., *el amor, la paz, el lápiz*).

 ¡LEE Y ESCRIBE!

When you write, here's how to change words from masculine to feminine:

man	*el señor*	woman	*la señora*
male teachers	*los profesores*	female teachers	*las profesoras*
male cat	*el gato*	female cat	*la gata*

You'll also need to know which words change in spelling when you make them plural:

baby	*el bebé*	pencil	*el lápiz*
babies	*los bebés*	pencils	*las lápices*

THE WORDS *UN* AND *UNA*

To say "a" or "an" in Spanish, you'll need the indefinite articles (*los artículos indefinidos*). Use *un* for masculine words or *una* for feminine words. They are also found everywhere:

A boy	*Un niño*	A girl	*Una niña*
A book	*Un libro*	A chair	*Una silla*

The words *uno*, *un*, and *una* can also mean "one" in English, so you may have to listen closely. And to say "some" in Spanish, use *unos* or *unas*:

Some boys	*Unos niños*	Some girls	*Unas niñas*
Some books	*Unos libros*	Some chairs	*Unas sillas*

¡PALABRAS EXTRAS!

These words also mean "some":

some man	*algún hombre*
some men	*algunos hombres*
some woman	*alguna mujer*
some women	*algunas mujeres*

 ## *¿Quieres Practicar?*

a.) Stick either *el* or *la* in front of these words:

1. ___ *carro*

2. ___ *fiesta*

3. ___ *señora*

4. ___ *computadora*

5. ___ *dinero*

b.) Translate:

1. *Unos apartamentos, una casa y un restaurante*

1. Some apartments, one/a house, and one/a restaurant

1. *el*   2. *la*   3. *la*   4. *la*   5. *el*

THE NUMBERS

Your Spanish class and textbook are filled with numbers, so practice them all day long—from saying page numbers to telling friends the date or time. Start by counting one to twenty now:

0	*cero*	11	*once*
1	*uno*	12	*doce*
2	*dos*	13	*trece*
3	*tres*	14	*catorce*
4	*cuatro*	15	*quince*
5	*cinco*	16	*dieciséis*
6	*seis*	17	*diecisiete*
7	*siete*	18	*dieciocho*
8	*ocho*	19	*diecinueve*
9	*nueve*	20	*veinte*
10	*diez*		

Twenty-one to twenty-nine are usually written as one long word:

21	*veintiuno*	26	*veintiséis*
22	*veintidós*	27	*veintisiete*
23	*veintitrés*	28	*veintiocho*
24	*veinticuatro*	29	*veintinueve*
25	*veinticinco*		

The numbers 30 to 90 end in *-nta* while 200 to 900 end in *-ientos*:

30	*treinta*	100	*cien*
40	*cuarenta*	200	*doscientos*
50	*cincuenta*	300	*trescientos*
60	*sesenta*	400	*cuatrocientos*
70	*setenta*	500	*quinientos*
80	*ochenta*	600	*seiscientos*
90	*noventa*	700	*setecientos*
		800	*ochocientos*
		900	*novecientos*

1.000 *mil*
1.000.000 *un millón*

Check out these examples of how to use numbers. See how they must match in gender, too:

542 women	*quinientas cuarenta y dos mujeres*
398 men	*trescientos noventa y ocho hombres*
760,000 people	*setecientas sesenta mil personas*

> Who said you'd ace Spanish by not doing anything? It takes serious study time, especially if you want to learn the language quickly!

 ¿Quieres Practicar?

Translate:

1. Eight friends   *ocho amigos*

2. 200 cars

3. 150 houses

4. 73 books

5. 16 chocolates

5. *dieciséis chocolates*
4. *setenta y tres libros*
3. *ciento cincuenta casas*
2. *doscientos carros*

QUANTITY WORDS

Since we're talking about numbers, why not mix in a word or two that expresses quantity. These words are constantly repeated:

only	*sólo*	*sólo uno*
a lot (of it)	*mucho*	*mucho dinero*
a lot (of them)	*muchos*	*muchos amigos*
small amount	*poco*	*poco trabajo*
few	*pocos*	*pocos adultos*
several	*varios*	*varios estudiantes*
all (of it)	*todo*	*todo el papel*
none	*ninguno*	*ninguno de los niños*
each	*cada*	*cada momento*

both	*ambos*	*ambos profesores*
all (of them)	*todos*	*todos los días*
so much	*tanto*	*tanto amor*
too much	*demasiado*	*demasiado pan*
the rest	*los demás*	*los demás libros*

Folks are always making references to quantites:

something	*algo*	*¿Necesita algo Ud.?*
anything	*cualquier cosa*	*Cualquier cosa, avísame.*
nothing	*nada*	*Nada es imposible.*
everything	*todo*	*Y todo es posible.*
someone	*alguien*	*Alguién está en el baño.*
anyone	*cualquier persona*	*Practico español con cualquier persona.*
no one	*nadie*	*Nadie está en la oficina.*
everyone	*todo el mundo*	*Todo el mundo habla inglés.*

¡SECRETOS!

The ordinal numbers below are also popular words for students. Spanish speakers use them all the time, so impress others by saying a phrase or two related to your school:

1st	1°	*primero*	*¡Soy el primero!* (I'm the first one!)
2nd	2°	*segundo*	*Es mi segunda clase.* (It's my second class.)
3rd	3°	*tercero*	*El tercero es difícil.* (The third one is difficult.)
4th	4°	*cuarto*	*Rita está en su cuarto año.* (Rita is in her 4th year.)
5th	5°	*quinto*	_____
6th	6°	*sexto*	_____
7th	7°	*séptimo*	_____
8th	8°	*octavo*	_____
9th	9°	*noveno*	_____
10th	10°	*décimo*	_____

¿Quieres Practicar?

Write in the opposite:

1. *mucha* _____   4. *varios* _____

2. *algo* _____   5. *nadie* _____

3. *todos* _____

1. poca   2. nada   3. ninguno   4. pocos   5. alguien

WORDS THAT TELL "WHEN"

Keep listening for any words related to time. Never forget that it's okay to answer a simple question with a single word or two:

When does he arrive?	*¿Cuándo llega?*
before	*antes*
after	*después*
now	*ahora*
never	*nunca*
always	*siempre*
sometimes	*a veces*
soon	*pronto*
later	*luego*
early	*temprano*
late	*tarde*
immediately	*immediatamente*

Remember that these frequently used words, the days and months, are never capitalized:

lunes	Monday
	A veces hay examen los <u>lunes</u>.
	Sometimes there's an exam on Mondays.
martes	Tuesday
miércoles	Wednesday
jueves	Thursday
viernes	Friday
sábado	Saturday
domingo	Sunday

enero	January
	Siempre hay fiesta en <u>enero</u>.
	There's always a party in January.
febrero	February
marzo	March
abril	April
mayo	May
junio	June
julio	July
agosto	August
septiembre	September
octubre	October
noviembre	November
diciembre	December

¡LEE Y ESCRIBE!

Careful! The date in Spanish reads like this—backwards:

July 4, 2014 = *el cuatro de julio, dos mil catorce*

In numbers, it's also reversed:

July 4, 2014 = 4-7-14

¿Quieres Practicar?

a.) Fill in the missing words:

1. *enero, febrero, _____, abril, mayo, _____ , julio, _____,*

   septiembre, _____, _____, diciembre

2. _____, *martes, miércoles,* _____, *viernes, sábado,* _____

b.) Guess what these words mean:

1. *antes de la fiesta*

2. *después de la conferencia*

3. *Siempre hablo español.*

3. I always speak Spanish.
2. after the meeting
1. before the party

2. *lunes, jueves, domingo*
1. *marzo, junio, agosto, octubre, noviembre*

¡PALABRAS EXTRAS!

Instead of learning new words separately, try focusing on them as parts of a longer phrase. You should be able to create some without any help:

since	*desde*	*desde ayer*
until	*hasta*	*hasta mañana*
end	*fin*	*a fin de año*
beginning	*principios*	*a principios de la semana*
in the middle	*mediados*	*a mediados del mes*

¡SECRETOS!

In Spain and Latin America, people find better things to do than stare at a clock all day. School schedules and time constraints are a bit more flexible, so discussing the time isn't always detailed, specific, or precise.

WORDS THAT TELL "WHERE"

The most popular response to the question *¿Dónde?* (Where?) is *en . . .* (in, on, at . . .): *Juan está <u>en</u> la clase, <u>en</u> la silla y <u>en</u> la mesa.* (Juan is in the class, on the chair, and at the table.) Point as you practice:

He's . . .	*Está . . .*
right here	*aquí*
over there	*allí*
there, near you	*ahí*
way over there	*allá*

¡OYE!

The tiny word *de* basically means "of" or "from" in English. It is also used in hundreds of other phrases and expressions where it can't really be translated. It's best to learn each of those one-liners as a whole! Also remember that *de* + *el* = *del: Carlos está enfrente del carro.* (Carlos is in front of the car.)

Keep it simple by learning a few words a day:

in front	*enfrente*	next to	*al lado*
in back	*atrás*	between	*entre*
forward	*adelante*	in the center	*en el medio*
behind	*detrás*	beside	*junto a*
under	*debajo*	outside	*afuera*
over	*sobre*	inside	*adentro*
up	*arriba*	near	*cerca*
down	*abajo*	far	*lejos*

to the right	*a la derecha*
to the left	*a la izquierda*
straight ahead	*de frente/recto/*
	derecho
on top	*encima*

¿Quieres Practicar?

Connect the words with opposite meanings:

1. *aquí*   *lejos*
2. *arriba*   *allí*
3. *detrás*   *derecha*
4. *cerca*   *abajo*
5. *izquierda* *enfrente*

1. *aquí*   *allí*
2. *arriba*   *abajo*
3. *detrás*   *enfrente*
4. *cerca*   *lejos*
5. *izquierda* *derecha*

¡CONVERSEMOS!

If you want to give directions, this little command word will do wonders:

Go . . .	Vaya . . .	*Vaya a la derecha.*	*Vaya arriba.*
		No vaya a la izquierda.	*No vaya abajo.*

¡LEE Y ESCRIBE!

As you know, Spanish generally uses more words to express the exact same thing as English. Look at these:

everywhere	*por todos lados*	nowhere	*en ninguna parte*
anywhere	*en cualquier lugar*	somewhere	*en alguna parte*

THE QUESTION WORDS

"Question" words are also used repeatedly, especially in simple conversations:

How many?	*¿Cuántos?*	*¿Cuántos años tiene Ud.?*
How much?	*¿Cuánto?*	*¿Cuánto cuesta?*
How?	*¿Cómo?*	*¿Cómo está Ud.?*
What?	*¿Qué?*	*¿Qué pasa?*
Where?	*¿Dónde?*	*¿Dónde está el baño?*
Which or What?	*¿Cuál?*	*¿Cuál es su nombre?*
When?	*¿Cuándo?*	*¿Cuándo es la clase?*
Who?	*¿Quién?*	*¿Quién es su amigo?*
Whose?	*¿De quién?*	*¿De quién es el libro?*
Why?	*¿Por qué?*	*¿Por qué estudia español Ud.?*

To get an A+ in Spanish, your response to simple questions must be automatic. By focusing on the initial word, and then listening for any key words that follow, you should be able to grasp what the fast-talking Spanish speaker is asking:

QUESTION	RESPONSE
¿Cuándo . . . blah,blah,blah . . . Halloween?	(Chances are, *octubre* is part of the answer.)
¿Dónde . . . blah,blah,blah . . . los Rockies?	(And what state in the United States comes to mind here?)

 ## *¿Quieres Practicar?*

Match the question words with the answers:

1. *¿Cuántos?*	*Roberto*
2. *¿Dónde?*	*Dos*
3. *¿Quién?*	*Mucho*
4. *¿Cuándo?*	*Florida*
5. *¿Cuánto?*	*El cinco de mayo*

1. *Dos*   2. *Florida*   3. *Roberto*   4. *El cinco de mayo*   5. *Mucho*

EVERYDAY WORDS

To raise your grade in Spanish, know this vocabulary well! Try to make up a sample sentence:

THINGS	*LAS COSAS*	
book	*el libro*	*¿Dónde está mi libro?*
phone	*el teléfono*	
chair	*la silla*	*No es su silla.*
classroom	*el salón de clase*	
clothing	*la ropa*	
computer	*la computadora*	
desk	*el escritorio*	
door	*la puerta*	*La puerta está allí.*
floor	*el piso*	*¿Cuál piso?*
food	*la comida*	
homework	*la tarea*	*La tarea es para mañana.*
lunch	*el almuerzo*	
office	*la oficina*	*Vaya a la oficina.*
paper	*el papel*	
pen	*el lapicero*	
pencil	*el lápiz*	
restroom	*el baño*	
room	*el cuarto*	*Necesito el número del cuarto.*
school	*la escuela*	
table	*la mesa*	
trash basket	*el cesto de basura*	
whiteboard	*el pizarrón*	
window	*la ventana*	

¡OYE!

Write the Spanish names of common objects with a black marker on sticky notes and place them in plain sight. As you walk by the objects later, call out the names of everything you see!

Identify these people in Spanish whenever you see them:

PEOPLE	*LA GENTE*
kids	*los niños*
friends	*los amigos*
men	*los hombres*
women	*las mujeres*
young people	*los muchachos/los chicos/los jóvenes*
students	*los estudiantes/los alumnos*
teachers	*los maestros/los profesores*

FAMILY	*LA FAMILIA*
father	*el padre*
mother	*la madre*
husband	*el esposo*
wife	*la esposa*
son	*el hijo*
daughter	*la hija*
brother	*el hermano*
sister	*la hermana*

Learn descriptive words by listing them as opposites:

DESCRIPTIONS	*LAS DESCRIPCIONES*	DESCRIPTIONS	*LAS DESCRIPCIONES*
bad	*malo/a*	good	*bueno/a*
big	*grande*	small	*pequeño/a*
short (length)	*corto/a*	long	*largo/a*
new	*nuevo/a*	old	*viejo/a*
pretty	*bonito/a*	ugly	*feo/a*
short (height)	*bajo/a*	tall	*alto/a*

Some students learn words through word association techniques:

COLORS	*LOS COLORES*	
white	*blanco/a*	This <u>white</u> paper is *blanco* (blank).
yellow	*amarillo/a*	The <u>yellow</u> sun shines over *Amarillo*, Texas.
brown	*café*	This <u>brown</u> stain is where I spilled my *café* (coffee).
red	*rojo/a*	
gray	*gris*	
green	*verde*	
orange	*anaranjado/a*	
purple	*morado/a*	
black	*negro/a*	
blue	*azul*	

¿Quieres Practicar?

a.) Fill in the words that have opposite meanings:

1. *blanco* _____   4. *bueno* _____

2. *alto* _____   5. *las mujeres* _____

3. *padre* _____

5. *los hombres*   4. *malo*   3. *madre*   2. *bajo*   1. *negro*

b.) Read these words aloud:

Los hombres son guapos y altos.
El piso en el salón de clase es blanco y negro.
Los nuevos estudiantes están en la mesa grande.

¡PALABRAS EXTRAS!

To learn more descriptions (descriptive adjectives), pair each one with its opposite. Look how the endings change based on gender:

fat	*gordo/a*	thin	*delgado/a*
strong	*fuerte*	weak	*débil*
dirty	*sucio/a*	clean	*limpio/a*
slow	*lento/a*	fast	*rápido/a*
easy	*fácil*	difficult	*difícil*
cold	*frío/a*	hot	*caliente*

¡LEE Y ESCRIBE!

Here's a quick tip for using colors and other descriptive adjectives—
THINK BACKWARDS! The descriptive word goes after the word being described:

The big house	*La casa grande*
The green chair	*La silla verde*
The important man	*El hombre importante*

And when you talk in plurals, not only do all the nouns and adjectives need to end in *s* or *es* to make the sentence plural, but when they are used together, the genders (the *o*'s and *a*'s), must match as well:

Two white doors	*Dos puertas blancas*
Many red cars	*Muchos carros rojos*
Six little children	*Seis niños pequeños*

COMMAND WORDS

Remember that the formal commands listed here differ from the familiar ones. Commands are heard wherever you go:

SPANISH			
(Formal)	**(Informal)**	**ENGLISH**	**SAMPLE SENTENCE**
Vaya	*Ve*	Go	*Vaya a María.*
Venga	*Ven*	Come	*Venga a la clase.*
Abra	*Abre*	Open	*Abra el libro.*
Cierre	*Cierra*	Close	*Cierre la puerta.*
Prenda	*Prende*	Turn on	*Prenda la luz.*
Apague	*Apaga*	Turn off	*Apague la computadora.*
Escuche	*Escucha*	Listen	*Escuche la música.*
Hable	*Habla*	Speak	*Hable más despacio.*
Lea	*Lee*	Read	*Lea el papel.*
Escriba	*Escribe*	Write	*Escriba su nombre.*

To give an order to more than one person, such as to a class, simply add the letter *n* to these words. Look at the examples and finish filling in the rest of these blanks before you look at the sentences in the last column.

PERSON		**GROUP**	
Diga	Tell or Say	*Digan*	*Digan hola a la maestra.*
Pregunte	Ask	*Pregunten*	*Pregunten en español.*
Siga	Follow or Continue	_____	*Sigan las instrucciones.*
Guarde	Put away	_____	*Guarden sus cosas.*
Tome	Take	_____	*Tomen los lapiceros.*
Escoja	Choose	_____	*Escojan una mesa.*
Estudie	Study	_____	*Estudien para el examen.*

¡CONVERSEMOS!

Listen for these four Spanish words that go with the commands:

this	*este*	*Abran este libro.*	that	*ese*	*Miren ese papel.*
	esta	*Escriba esta letra.*		*esa*	*Siéntese en esa silla.*

¿Quieres Practicar?

Follow these simple commands:

1. *Cierre este libro.*

2. *Escriba su nombre en un papel.*

3. *Diga su número de teléfono en español.*

STEP THREE: LIST THOSE WORDS THAT ARE DIFFICULT TO REMEMBER.

SCHOOL WORDS

A+ Spanish students must also have their lists of difficult vocabulary. To create one, check "OK" if a word is relatively simple for you or "HARD" if it's one that looks like trouble. Start with words you need for school:

		OK	HARD
library	*la biblioteca*	_____	_____
hall	*el corredor*	_____	_____
gym	*el gimnasio*	_____	_____
cafeteria	*cafetería*	_____	_____
building	*el edificio*	_____	_____
parking	*el estacionamiento*	_____	_____
counselor	*el consejero/la consejera*	_____	_____
librarian	*el bibliotecario/la bibliotecaria*	_____	_____

Separate the names of things from those that refer to people:

PEOPLE	(LA GENTE)
nurse	*el enfermero/la enfermera*
principal	*el director/la directora*
vice principal	*el subdirector/la subdirectora*
security guard	*el guardia/la guardia*
secretary	*el secretario/la secretaria*

THINGS   *(LAS COSAS)*

bookcase	*el librero*	backpack	*la mochila*
bulletin board	*el tablero*	dictionary	*el diccionario*
cabinet	*el gabinete*	eraser	*el borrador*
carpet	*la alfombra*	folder	*la carpeta*
clock	*el reloj*	marker	*el marcador*
file cabinet	*el archivero*	notebook	*el cuaderno*
light	*la luz*	scissors	*las tijeras*
map	*el mapa*	sheet of paper	*la hoja de papel*
projector	*el proyector*	stapler	*la grapadora*
seat	*el asiento*	textbook	*el libro de texto*
shelf	*el estante*		

¡OYE!

There are countless ways to learn new vocabulary:

- Group the words in a way that makes sense to you
- Hear each word, say it aloud, then read and write it carefully
- Picture what each word means and repeat it several times
- Point to the named object or touch it as you say its name aloud
- Make Spanish-English vocabulary flashcards on index cards
- Practice with a Spanish vocabulary online tool or download

¡SECRETOS!

Teachers and textbooks differ slightly in how they name certain items, so do not panic if a word on this list might not be used in your classroom. It's usually because of a cultural difference. Simply add the one you are taught, and remember that eventually you'll come across the one in this book (and perhaps others) out there in the vast world of international Spanish communications.

¿Quieres Practicar?

Delete the word from each list that doesn't belong with the others:

1. *guardia, maestro, escritorio, director*

2. *lápiz, papel, pluma, edificio*

3. *luz, mochila, gabinete, asiento*

SPANISH STUDENT WORDS

From the moment you started learning Spanish, you have been bombarded with foreign vocabulary. Try writing down the more difficult words twice:

accent	*el acento*	_____	_____
alphabet	*el abecedario*	*el abecedario*	*el abecedario*
answer	*la respuesta*	*la respuesta*	*la respuesta*
chapter	*el capítulo*	_____	_____
culture	*la cultura*	_____	_____
exercise	*el ejercicio*	_____	_____
grammar	*la gramática*	_____	_____
language	*el lenguaje/el idioma*	_____	_____
page	*la página*	_____	_____
pronunciation	*la pronunciación*	_____	_____
question	*la pregunta*	_____	_____
quiz	*la prueba*	_____	_____
review	*el repaso*	_____	_____
sentence	*la oración, la frase*	_____	_____
exam	*el examen*	_____	_____
word	*la palabra*	_____	_____

¡LEE Y ESCRIBE!

Be careful with making translations! An online translation tool offers a good guide, and is very helpful to get a broad understanding of a word, but should never be relied upon as 100% accurate.

¿Quieres Practicar?

Without checking, can you translate these words correctly? They're not easy to remember!

1. *la palabra* _____
2. *la oración* _____
3. *la pregunta* _____
4. *el idioma* _____
5. *la respuesta* _____

1. word   2. sentence   3. question   4. language   5. answer

¡PALABRAS EXTRAS!

English dominates the cyber-world, so don't fret if you forget a "computer" word. Here's what most Spanish speakers say:

el laptop	*el website*	*el i-phone*	*la internet*
el e-book	*la Skype*	*la texting*	*la web-cam*

¡CONVERSEMOS!

To learn these words quickly, ask your instructor about setting up communication with exchange students from Spain or Latin America. Better yet, find a local tutor or fluent Spanish speaker who will practice with you by email or through Skype.

Another suggestion is to practice those words that relate to something that really interests you. If you're into sports, music, or perhaps a hobby, begin with a list there. While you're at it, try a technique called mnemonics (new-MAH-nix), which is a technique to improve memorization. All you need is a creative formula, mental image, or rhyme:

SPANISH	ENGLISH	PICTURE
zorro	fox	A fox dressed in the mask of *Zorro*.
luz	light	A lightbulb that is *loose*.
enero	January	A January calendar with *an arrow* in it.
silla	chair	A chair falling off a cliff saying, "*See ya!*"
mujer	woman	A woman saying, "I want *more hair.*"
sopa	soup	A bowl of soup full of *soap*.

¡OYE!

Write down words that you have difficulty pronouncing or seem to forget, but avoid those you seldom use. Only work on those that you know you're going to need to socialize or complete a class assignment.

COMPOUND WORDS

In Spanish, a compound word may look difficult, but it's easy to memorize once you cut it in half. They are actually two separate words in one:

dishwasher	*lavaplatos*	*lava* (wash) *platos* (dishes)
skyscraper	*rascacielos*	*rasca* (scrape) *cielos* (skies)
can opener	*abrelatas*	*abre* (open) *latas* (cans)
nail cutters	*cortauñas*	*corta* (cut) *uñas* (nails)
windshield wipers	*limpiaparabrisas*	*limpia* (cleans) *parabrisas* (windshield)

Some compound words require a little more imagination, because the actual meaning isn't precise. The line shows where the two words come together, yet express a complete sentence:

SPANISH WORD	MEANING	LITERAL TRANSLATION
espanta/pájaros	scarecrow	It scares/birds.
lava/manos	bathroom sink	It washes/hands.
para/caídas	parachute	It stops/falls.
para/choques	bumper	It stops/crashes.
salva/vidas	life preserver	It saves/lives.

> None of this matters if you don't do the *¿Quieres practicar?* sections.
> All this information won't stick if it's not put into practice!

¿Quieres Practicar?

Choose one of the methods you've learned in this chapter and use it to memorize a few difficult Spanish words. Simply go to an online Spanish dictionary, pick out three words you've never seen before, and give the method a try. And when you're done, do the same thing again, but by using a different approach!

¡LEE Y ESCRIBE!

Everything goes well with the little word *Hay* (pronounced "I") in Spanish. It can mean "There is" or "There are":

There's one chair.	*Hay una silla.*
Are there lots of students?	*¿Hay muchos estudiantes?*
There is no table.	*No hay una mesa.*
Aren't there any women?	*¿No hay mujeres?*

THE CONNECTING VERBS

Some hard-to-remember Spanish words are those that help to form a complete sentence. These include the linking verbs *SER, ESTAR,* and *TENER.* Their forms are in the present tense:

TO BE → ESTAR (when referring to location or a temporary condition)		TO BE → SER (when referring to a characteristic or quality)	
I am . . .	*Estoy . . .*	*Soy . . .*	*Estoy bien. Soy Juan.*
You are . . . (sing. inf.)	*Estás . . .*	*Eres . . .*	*Estás aquí. Eres alta.*
You are . . . (sing. form.)	*Está . . .*	*Es . . .*	*Está feliz. Es bonita.*
He, She, It is . . .	*Está . . .*	*Es . . .*	*Está sucio. Es viejo.*
We are . . .	*Estamos . . .*	*Somos . . .*	_____
*You are . . . (pl. inf.)	*Estáis . . .*	*Sois . . .*	_____
You are . . . (pl. form.)	*Están . . .*	*Son . . .*	_____
They are . . .	*Están . . .*	*Son . . .*	_____

*These are used in Spain only. *Están, Son,* and *Tienen* are used in Latin America instead.

TO HAVE	*TENER*	
I have . . .	*Tengo* . . .	*Tengo hambre.* (I'm hungry.)
You have . . . (sing. inf.)	*Tienes* . . .	*Tienes sed.* (You're thirsty.)
You have . . . (sing. form.)	*Tiene* . . .	*Tiene frío.* (You're cold.)
He, She, It has . . .	*Tiene* . . .	*Tiene calor.* (She's hot.)
We have . . .	*Tenemos* . . .	
*You have . . . (pl. inf.)	*Tenéis* . . .	
You have . . . (pl. form.)	*Tienen* . . .	
They have . . .	*Tienen* . . .	

The abbreviations above for "singular informal" (**sing. inf.**) and "plural informal" (**pl. inf.**) verb forms are used with close friends, family, and children. The abbreviations (**sing. form.**) and (**pl. form.**) refer to the formal verb forms, and are used with others as a sign of respect. You'll also notice that words like *Yo* (I), *Tú* (You, **sing. inf.**), *Él* (He), and *Ella* (She) are not included in a sentence, unless there is some confusion about who is involved.

¿Quieres Practicar?

Translate these words into English:

1. *Tienes* _____

2. *Estamos* _____

3. *Soy* _____

4. *Tenemos* _____

5. *Están* _____

1. You have (inf. sing.)
2. We are
3. I am
4. We have
5. They, You (pl.) are

*These are not used frequently. *Están, Son,* and *Tienen* are used instead.

LITTLE SPANISH WORDS

Some of the hardest words for Spanish students to remember are not the longer ones, but those that are often overlooked. Let's divide this section of little words into three groups—ONE-LETTER, TWO-LETTER, and THREE-LETTER words:

ONE-LETTER WORDS

You can't skip these no matter how small they appear:

o, u = or	(*o* changes to *u* before *o-* or *ho-*)	*¿Tacos o tamales? ¿María u Olivia?*
a = to	(or add *a* if addressing a person)	*¡Vamos a la clase! Invita a Juan.*
y, i = and	(*y* changes to *e* before *i-* or *hi-*)	*Hay dinero y amor. Son padre e hijo.*

¡CONVERSEMOS!

Pero and *sino* both mean "but" in English, yet are used quite differently. *Sino* actually means "but, rather." Look:

Quiero los tacos, <u>pero</u> no quiero la salsa.
I want the tacos, <u>but</u> I don't want the salsa.

No quiero los tamales, <u>sino</u> los tacos.
I don't want the tamales, <u>but</u> (rather) the tacos.

TWO-LETTER WORDS

It's hard to say anything in Spanish without including one of these. Read each sentence aloud:

al	to the (*a + el = al*)	*Vamos al restaurante.*
de	of or from	*Carlos es de Cuba.*
el	the (masculine)	*Necesito el carro.*
él	he	*Cecilia y él son amigos.*
en	in, on, at	*Está en la casa.*
es	it is, he is, she is, you are (sing. form.)	*El hospital es grande.*
la	the (feminine)	*¿Dónde está la fiesta?*
no	no	*Antonio no es doctor.*
si	if	*Invita a Juan si está en la casa.*
sí	yes	*Sí, trabajo mucho.*
un	a (masculine)	*Un café grande, por favor.*
yo	I	*Yo estoy bien, gracias.*
ir	to go	*Es importante ir a la escuela.*

¡LEE Y ESCRIBE!

Several "little words" in Spanish are the pronouns, which are usually found on a chart, much like the one below. Don't worry about what all the little words mean or how to use them just yet. For now, simply try to remember that when you run into a "little word," chances are it's referring to a person or thing:

yo	me	me	me	mí	mí
tú	te	te	te	ti	ti
usted [Ud.]		lo, la		usted [Ud.]	
él	le	lo	se	él	sí
ella		la		ella	
nosotros, -as	nos	nos	nos	nosotros, -as	nosotros, -as
vosotros, -as	os	os	os	vosotros, -as	vosotros, -as
ustedes [Uds.]		los, las		ustedes [Uds.]	
ellos	les	los	se	ellos	sí
ellas		las		ellas	
= I, you, he, she, it, we, you, they	= to me, to you, to him, to her, to it, to us, to you, to them	= me, you, him, her, it, us, you, them	= myself, yourself, himself, herself, itself, ourselves, your-selves, them-selves	= [e.g., from] me, you, him, her, it, us, you, them	= [e.g., from] myself, your-self, himself, herself, itself, ourselves, yourselves, themselves

How's your positive mindset? You will not get an
A+ in Spanish unless you actually believe it's possible!

THREE-LETTER WORDS

Notice how many you know already! Be sure to jot down any word you're not familiar with:

año	year	*¿Qué pasó en el año 1776?*
con	with	*El estudiante está con el profesor.*
dar	to give	*Es importante dar agua a la planta.*
del	of the/from the	*La medicina es del doctor.*
día	day	*¿Qué día es mañana?*
dos	two	*Dos y dos son cuatro.*
eso	that	*¿Qué es eso?*
feo	ugly	*El sofá es muy feo.*
fin	end	*La lista está al fin del libro.*
hay	there is/there are	*Hay dos niños en la mesa.*
hoy	today	*Hoy es el cinco de mayo.*
luz	light	*Hay mucha luz en la clase.*
mal	ill/poorly	*El paciente está muy mal.*
mes	month	*Diciembre es mi mes favorito.*
muy	very	*Laura es muy inteligente.*
pan	bread	*El pan es delicioso.*
pie	foot	*¡No ponga los pies en la silla!*
por	by/through	*El Cid no fue escrito por Cervantes.*
sin	without	*Robert habla sin acento.*
sol	sun	*No hay mucho sol hoy.*
uno	one	*El número de mi apartamento es uno-dos-uno.*

¡OYE!

Abbreviations are short words, too. You've seen a few of them already, so you should know what they mean in English:

Mr.	*Sr.*	*Señor*
Mrs.	*Sra.*	*Señora*
Miss	*Srta.*	*Señorita*
You (sing. form.)	*Ud. or Vd.*	*Usted*
You (plu. form.)	*Uds. or Vds.*	*Ustedes*
United States (USA)	*E.E. U.U.*	*Los Estados Unidos*

¿Quieres Practicar?

How many two- or three-letter Spanish words do you know by heart? Write down some that begin with the following letters:

d   del, de, dar, _____

l   la, leo, _____

s   sol, _____

p   _____

m   _____

HOW TO GET AN A+

One of biggest barriers to learning Spanish is trying to remember all the vocabulary needed to express an immediate thought, opinion, or idea. Thankfully, this process is far less painful for those who follow these three important guidelines:

Step One: Focus on words that are **SIMILAR** to English or are relatively easy to remember.

Step Two: Learn those words that are **REPEATED** time and again in daily conversation.

Step Three: List those words that are **DIFFICULT** to remember and practice them every day.

Now it's time to create complete sentences, instead of mere phrases or expressions. To do so, we'll need the rules for putting our Spanish words together.

Chapter 4
Capítulo Cuatro

Grammar—Part One
La Gramática—Primera Parte

THE SENTENCE

Just as it is in English, a sentence (*oración*) in Spanish is an organized sequence of words that expresses a complete thought. Obviously, to get an A+ in Spanish, you have to speak and write in complete sentences.

I. Sentences: Three Main Types

The three main sentence types are identical to those in English:

1. DECLARATIVE (Makes a statement)   *Tengo el libro.*   I have the book.
2. INTERROGATIVE (Asks a question)   *¿Dónde está Lupe?*   Where's Lupe?
3. IMPERATIVE (Gives a command)   *¡Venga a la clase!*   Come to class!

¡LEE Y ESCRIBE!

An INTERROGATIVE sentence is always written in Spanish with a question mark at the end and an inverted mark at the beginning: *¿Cómo se llama Ud.?* (What's your name?). An IMPERATIVE or "emphatic" sentence comes in many forms, but may be written with an exclamation mark at the end and an inverted mark at the beginning: *¡Cierre la puerta!* (Close the door!).

II. Sentences: Subject and Predicate

Remember that sentences consist of two basic parts: the SUBJECT (noun or pronoun and its modifiers), and the PREDICATE (verb and its modifiers). As a rule, the SUBJECT begins a sentence, telling who or what is involved, while the PREDICATE provides information about the SUBJECT and includes the verb.

SUBJECT   PREDICATE
El estudiante habla con el profesor.
(The student talks with the professor.)

In Spanish, however, the PREDICATE may also <u>precede</u> the SUBJECT, which is why it sounds a little "backwards" at times. But regardless of the word order, your sentence still requires two main parts:

PREDICATE   SUBJECT
Habla con el profesor el estudiante.
(The student talks with the professor.)

¿Quieres Practicar?

Explain and then give one example of each of the following:

1. DECLARATIVE sentence:

   _____

2. INTERROGATIVE sentence:

   _____

3. IMPERATIVE sentence:

   _____

4. The SUBJECT of a sentence:

   _____

5. The PREDICATE of a sentence:

   _____

> **¡CONVERSEMOS!**
>
> The SUBJECT of a sentence generally consists of a noun, a noun phrase, or a pronoun. In Spanish, however, the English pronoun subject "it" does not have an equivalent. Notice how the meaning is implied by the verb:
>
> | | |
> |---|---|
> | *Es mío.* | It is mine. |
> | *Cuesta muy poquito.* | It costs very little. |
> | *Hace mucho frío.* | It is very cold. |

III. Sentences: Affirmative and Negative

Most sentences in Spanish are direct or "affirmative" statements, which express thoughts in a straightforward manner:

Manuel vive en Miami.	Manuel lives in Miami.
Me gusta el chocolate.	I like chocolate.

A negative sentence expresses the opposite message of an affirmative sentence. To form a negative statement in Spanish, simply place the word *no* before the predicate of an affirmative statement:

Manuel no vive en Miami.   Manuel doesn't live in Miami.

No me gusta el chocolate.   I don't like chocolate.

¡SECRETOS!

There's also something called an EXCLAMATORY SENTENCE in Spanish, which can be frequently used in everyday conversations. See how it "exclaims" a message instead of merely stating it:

¡No lo puedo creer!   I can't believe it!

¡Ella es tan bonita!   She is so pretty!

IV. Sentences: Clauses

No doubt you will also learn about CLAUSES in Spanish class. A CLAUSE is simply a group of related words containing a subject and a verb. To learn about the various types of CLAUSES, read each explanation below carefully, one section at a time:

A. The MAIN CLAUSE of a sentence generally contains the main or key subject and verb, while the added parts are called SUBORDINATE CLAUSES. That means you can also have a subordinate subject or predicate:

MAIN CLAUSE		SUBORDINATE CLAUSE		
Laura	*trabaja*	*porque*	*ella*	*necesita el dinero.*
(Laura)	(works)	(because)	(she)	(needs the money.)
MAIN SUBJ.	MAIN PRED.		SUB. SUBJ.	SUB. PRED.

MAIN CLAUSE = *Laura trabaja* + SUBORDINATE CLAUSE
SUBORDINATE CLAUSE = *porque ella necesita el dinero.*

B. A SUBORDINATE CLAUSE is sometimes called a DEPENDENT CLAUSE because in order to have meaning, it must depend on the information in the main clause. Notice how the DEPENDENT CLAUSE makes no sense all by itself:

DEPENDENT CLAUSE	MAIN CLAUSE
Si no llueve,	*voy a la clase.*
If it doesn't rain,	I'm going to class.

C. In contrast to the SUBORDINATE (DEPENDENT) CLAUSE, an INDEPENDENT CLAUSE may either stand alone by itself, or be attached to another INDEPENDENT CLAUSE by a coordinating conjunction (*y, o,* or *pero*). See how each CLAUSE expresses a complete thought or idea:

Voy a la clase.
I'm going to class.
INDEPENDENT CLAUSE

Voy a estudiar.
I'm going to study.
INDEPENDENT CLAUSE

Voy a la clase   *y*   *voy a estudiar.*
I'm going to class   and   I'm going to study.
INDEPENDENT CLAUSE   INDEPENDENT CLAUSE

¿Quieres Practicar?

Fill in the blanks with the correct word:

1. In contrast to the DEPENDENT CLAUSE, an _____ CLAUSE may either

   stand alone by itself, or be attached to another _____ CLAUSE.

2. The main subject and verb are often found in a _____ CLAUSE of a

   sentence, while the added parts are called _____ CLAUSES.

3. A SUBORDINATE CLAUSE is often called a _____ CLAUSE.

3. dependent
2. main, subordinate
1. independent, independent

V. Sentences: Direct and Indirect Objects

The predicate or "verb part" of a sentence may or may not have something called an OBJECT. For example, "*Ana es muy inteligente*" has no object. An object is basically a noun, pronoun, or noun phrase that is affected by the verb. Just remember that there are two main types of objects: DIRECT and INDIRECT. This is easy if you pay close attention:

A DIRECT OBJECT (D.O.) immediately follows the verb and receives the action the subject performs. It answers the question "what?" or "whom?" with regard to what the subject is doing:

Jaime	*lava*	*su carro.*	
Jaime	washes	his car.	(He washes what? His car = direct object)
SUBJ.	VERB	D.O.	

Now, underline the SUBJECT, VERB, and DIRECT OBJECT below:

Jaime	*entrega*	*su papel.*
Jaime	turns in	his paper.
SUBJ.	VERB	D.O.

An INDIRECT OBJECT (I.O.) may or may not follow the verb, and is basically the person or thing to whom or for whom the subject performs the action. It generally includes a pronoun and is introduced by the preposition *a*. See how the indirect object tells where a direct object is going and does not directly receive any action:

Jaime	*le*	*entrega*	*el papel*	*a*	*la maestra.*
Jaime	(to him)	turns in	the paper	to	the teacher.
SUBJ.		VERB	D.O.		I.O

Okay, you try one. Label the SUBJ., VERB, D.O., and I.O below. For now, don't be concerned about the little pronoun *le*:

Le ofrezco la fruta a mi amiga.
I offer fruit to my friend.

Whether the object of a sentence is DIRECT or INDIRECT often depends on the verb (action word). Some verbs must be followed by one type of object or the other. One of the best ways to know if the object is direct or indirect is to learn common verbs that require either a D.O. or I.O. Fortunately, most verbs in Spanish match their English equivalents when it comes to whether or not a direct or indirect object should follow. Follow the pattern in these examples:

USED WITH A D.O.

comer (to eat)   *Voy a comer el taco.* (I'm going to eat the taco.)
                                              D.O.

guardar (to put away)   *Voy a* _____

tomar (to take)   *Voy a* _____

calentar (to heat)   *Voy a* _____

USED WITH AN I.O.

dar (to give)   *Le voy a dar el taco a <u>Tina</u>.* (I'm going to give the taco to Tina.)
                                                   I.O.

mostrar (to show)   *Le voy a* _____

vender (to sell)   *Le voy a* _____

ofrecer (to offer)   *Le voy a* _____

Do not forget that most sentences in Spanish include both types of objects, and that sometimes the I.O. is not stated, but rather is implied or understood:

Le voy a dar	*rosas*	*(a mi amigo).*
I'm going to give	roses	(to my friend).
	D.O.	I.O.

¡PALABRAS EXTRAS!

This topic is a struggle for students, especially when it involves DIRECT AND INDIRECT OBJECT PRONOUNS. But, don't worry. You'll learn about them very soon:

<u>Nos</u> *venden la fruta.*	They sell fruit to <u>us</u>.
<u>Le</u> *dice la verdad.*	She tells the truth to <u>him</u>.
<u>Me lo</u> *trae.*	He brings <u>it</u> to <u>me</u>.

To sum up, the DIRECT OBJECT is who or what receives the action of the verb, while the INDIRECT OBJECT is generally who or what receives the direct object. Memorize this simple summary and you won't need to study the topic again!

Lost? Go back to the part where you understood everything,
and start reading all over again!

¿Quieres Practicar?

Write the D.O. and I.O. in each sentence below:

EXAMPLE: *Sofía le compra revistas a Juan.* (Sofía buys John magazines.)

                                    D.O.   I.O.

1. *Mi madre le lee el libro al niño.* (My mother reads the book to the child.)

2. *Paulo le muestra las fotos a la clase.* (Paulo shows photos to the class.)

3. *¿Le venden libros a Ud.?* (Do they sell books to you?)

4. *No le doy dulces a mi hermano.* (I don't give candy to my brother.)

5. *Le pagamos mucho dinero al doctor.* (We pay the doctor a lot of money.)

	D.O.	I.O.
1.	libro	niño
2.	fotos	la clase
3.	libros	Ud.
4.	dulces	hermano
5.	dinero	doctor

¡OYE!

Generally speaking, the basic interrogative, affirmative, and negative sentence forms in Spanish are easy to construct. Just remember that an affirmative statement is frequently converted into a question simply by raising one's voice slightly at the end:

Hablas español.	You speak Spanish.
¿Hablas español?	Do you speak Spanish?
No hablas español.	You don't speak Spanish.

VI. Sentences: Simple vs. Complex

Sentences either have a SIMPLE structure or they are considered COMPLEX. A simple sentence has one (main) subject and one (main) predicate that form the main clause:

SIMPLE
El hombre está manejando.
The man is driving.

A complex sentence has at least one other clause (subordinate) besides the main clause. Here are two examples:

COMPLEX:
El hombre que está manejando habla inglés.
The man who is driving speaks English.

Cuando está manejando, el hombre habla inglés.
The man speaks English when he's driving.

Look closely at the two COMPLEX sentences above. Students who can create sentences like these are the ones who get an A+ in Spanish class! The secret to doing so is in knowing how to use the words *que* and *cuando* in a sentence. Underline them in the sentences, and notice how they are part of a subordinate clause.

VII. Sentences: Relative and Temporal

There are two main types of subordinate clauses in Spanish. One is referred to as a RELATIVE CLAUSE, because it is introduced by a relative pronoun, such as *que*, which means "that, who, or which." Look how it works:

MAIN CLAUSE   RELATIVE CLAUSE
El hombre habla inglés.   +   *que está manejando*   =
       El hombre que está manejando habla inglés.

The other kind of subordinate clause is called a TEMPORAL CLAUSE because it is introduced by subordinating conjunctions that usually tell "*when*" and refer to time:

MAIN CLAUSE   TEMPORAL CLAUSE
el hombre habla inglés.   +   *Cuando está manejando,*   =
       Cuando está manejando, el hombre habla inglés.

Some subordinating conjunctions may also express "*where*" or "*why.*" Again, notice how the two clauses form a complex sentence:

Donde vive ella, hay menos tráfico.
Where she lives, there is less traffic.

Porque no se siente bien, el artista no puede venir.
Because he doesn't feel well, the artist can't come.

¿Quieres Practicar?

a.) Underline the sentences that are considered COMPLEX:

1. *La chica que baila bien trabaja en el café.*

2. *Voy a la escuela y estudio español.*

3. *Cuando la clase termina, vamos a la playa.*

4. *Es la casa que tiene dos puertas grandes.*

5. *Yo vivo cerca de muchos lagos muy bonitos.*

b.) Connect each grammatical term with its example:

1. subordinating conjunction   a. *cuando está hablando*

2. relative pronoun   b. *cuando*

3. temporal clause   c. *que habla mucho*

4. main clause   d. *el hombre habla*

5. relative clause   e. *que*

e. relative pronoun
d. main clause
c. relative clause
b. subordinating conjunction
a. temporal clause

4. *Es la casa que tiene dos puertas grandes.*
1. *La chica que baila bien trabaja en el café.*

¡LEE Y ESCRIBE!

Subordinating conjunctions introduce a subordinate or dependent clause [i.e., *cuando* (when), *donde* (where), and *porque* (because): *Cuando Ud. está aquí, estoy muy contento*]. However, when two or more independent clauses are joined together by a coordinating conjunction, it is called a "compound" sentence, not a "complex" one: *Como pan tostado y tomo café caliente cada día.*

Voy a mi casa y voy a comer algo, pero no voy a mirar televisión.
I'm going home and I'm going to eat something, but I'm not going to watch T.V.

So, what have you learned about creating sentences in Spanish? List all that you know below:

    I. Three Main Types:
   II. Subject and Predicate:
 III. Affirmative and Negative:
 IV. Clauses:
   V. Direct and Indirect Objects:
 VI. Simple and Complex:
VII. Relative and Temporal:

NOUNS

I. Nouns: Gender

Although you'll never guess correctly 100% of the time, there are a few tricks to finding the correct gender of a Spanish word. "THE BIG TEN" teaches gender—a few rules at a time:

GENDER: THE BIG TEN

1. The letters of the alphabet are feminine: *la "a," la "hache," la "i,"* etc.

2. Nouns ending in *-dad, -tad, -tud, -umbre, -ión, -cia, -sis, -itis, -nza, -ie, -ez,* or *-eza* are usually feminine: *la parálisis, la libertad, la esperanza, la unión, la importancia,* etc.

3. The names for the days, months, colors, numbers, languages, rivers, oceans, as well as foreign words are all masculine: *el lunes, el mayo, el rojo, el cinco, el inglés, el Mississippi, el Pacífico, el marketing,* etc.

4. Similarly, nouns ending in *-ma, -ambre, -or, -aje, -án,* or in a vowel that is stressed are usually masculine: *el problema, el hambre, el tractor, el garaje, el champú,* etc.

5. The names for most trees are masculine, but their fruit is generally feminine: *el palto → la palta* (avocado), *el olivo → la oliva* (olive), *el peral → la pera* (pear), etc.

6. Nouns referring to people that end in *-or, -és, -ón,* and *-ín* are generally masculine, and an *-a* is added to become feminine. There is no accent in the feminine form: *el director → la directora; el japonés → la japonesa, el bailarín → la bailarina,* etc.

7. Still other nouns are altered slightly when they change from the masculine to the feminine form: *el poeta → la poetisa, el rey → la reina, el héroe → la heroína, el tigre → la tigresa, el gallo → la gallina,* etc.

8. Some nouns that refer to people change their article but keep only one form: *el/la dentista, el/la estudiante, el/la líder, el/la profesional, el/la joven,* etc.

9. A few nouns apply to both females and males: *la persona* (person), *el pájaro* (bird), *la rata* (rat), etc.

10. Many words change meaning with a change in gender: *el papa* (pope) → *la papa* (potato); *la mañana* (morning) → *el mañana* (tomorrow); *el frente* (front) → *la frente* (forehead), etc.

¡CONVERSEMOS!

A noun that begins with a stressed *a* or *ha* is considered feminine, even though it takes the masculine article in the singular and the feminine article in the plural:

El agua está fría.   The water is cold.

Las aguas de Hawaii son lindas.   The Hawaiian seas are lovely.

¿Quieres Practicar?

a.) Indicate the gender of these nouns correctly by inserting *el* or *la*:

1. ____ *mapa*

2. ____ *cometa*

3. ____ *pasaporte*

4. ____ *rubí*

5. ____ *valor*

b.) Translate these nouns into English:

1. *la papa*   _____

2. *la mañana*   _____

3. *el naranjo*   _____

4. *el gallo*   _____

5. *la gallina*   _____

c.) Translate the following nouns into Spanish:

1. Spanish   _____

2. five   _____

3. artist   _____

4. Thursday   _____

5. chocolate   _____

1. el	1. potato	1. el español
2. el	2. morning	2. cinco
3. el	3. orange tree	3. el/la artista
4. el	4. rooster	4. el jueves
5. el	5. hen	5. el chocolate

II. Nouns: Number

As you did with gender, study THE BIG TEN insights related to learning about nouns and number in Spanish. Use your dictionary if you want to understand every word:

NUMBER: THE BIG TEN

1. Some nouns remain the same in both the singular and the plural. You'll have to memorize these: *el análisis → los análisis, el paraguas→los paraguas, el miércoles → los miércoles*, etc.

2. Other nouns are almost always used in the plural form: *las tenazas* (tongs), *los alicates* (pliers), *los anteojos* (eyeglasses), *las tijeras* (scissors), etc.

3. Nouns with a final stressed syllable generally have no accent mark in the plural: *el autobús → los autobuses, el francés → los franceses, el cartón → los cartones*, etc.

4. A few nouns actually add an accent mark in the plural: *el examen → los exámenes, el origen → los orígenes*, etc.

5. Some nouns shift their stress to another syllable in the plural form: *el régimen → los regímenes*, etc.

6. Nouns ending in *-í* or *-ú* add *-es* instead of *-s* in the plural: *el colibrí → los colibríes, el menú → los menúes*, etc.

7. Other spelling changes include those nouns ending in *-z*, which becomes *-ces* in the plural: *el lápiz → los lápices, una vez → dos veces*, etc.

8. The masculine noun in the plural often refers to males and females combined: *mis tíos* (my aunts and uncles), *los maestros* (the male and female teachers), etc.

9. There is no plural form for a proper name referring to a family: *los García* (the Garcias); however, a plural form is used when a group of people happen to have the same name: *muchos Garcías* (lots of Garcias).

10. Spanish often uses the singular when the plural is used in English: *Tienen su cheque.* (They have their paychecks.), etc.

Now, try to name rules from THE BIG TEN lists above!

 ## *¿Quieres Practicar?*

a.) Change these isolated words to their plural form:

1. *rey*   los reyes

2. *autobús*   _____

3. *sábado*   _____

4. *cruz*   _____

5. *examen*   _____

b.) Translate each noun into English:

1. *los menúes*   _____

2. *los anteojos*   _____

3. *los López*   _____

4. *los hijos*   _____

5. *los paraguas*   _____

1. menus
2. glasses
3. the López family
4. a family's children
5. umbrellas

2. *los autobuses*
3. *los sábados*
4. *las cruces*
5. *los exámenes*

¡OYE!

When two nouns are compared, use the formula *más/menos* _____ *que* (more/less _____ than):

Tengo más clases que mis amigos.
I have more classes than my friends.

When two nouns are compared as equals, use the word *tanto*. Notice how *tanto* must agree or match the noun it describes:

Tengo tantas clases como mis amigos.
I have as many classes as my friends.

ARTICLES

In this section, you'll learn about three different kinds of articles in Spanish, and how to use them correctly. The two most important are called DEFINITE and INDEFINITE, which were called DIFFICULT VOCABULARY earlier in the book.

I. Definite Article

Let's stick with "THE BIG TEN" list and study the definite article just a little at a time:

DEFINITE ARTICLE: THE BIG TEN

1. Definite articles are used with articles of clothing and parts of the body. Notice how English uses possessive pronouns instead: *Me voy a quitar la camisa.* (I'm going to take off my shirt.), *Le duelen los brazos.* (Her arms hurt.)

2. Definite articles are used with the time of day, the days of the week, and the seasons of the year. *A las tres* (at three), *los viernes* (on Fridays). Just remember that the definite article is not used with the days of the week when they follow the verb *SER*: *Hoy es lunes.* (Today is Monday.)

3. Definite articles are used with the names of mountains, rivers, and oceans: *Los Andes son muy bonitos.* (The Andes mountains are beautiful.), *Me gusta el río Colorado.* (I like the Colorado River.)

4. Definite articles are used before infinitives or adjectives that are used as nouns: *El correr es buen ejercicio.* (Running is good exercise.), *Quiero el más chico.* (I want the smallest one.)

5. Definite articles are used before titles of address followed by a proper name, except when the person is being spoken to directly: *La doctora Lara es mi amiga.* (Dr. Lara is my friend.), *¿Doctora Lara, qué hora es?* (Dr. Lara, what time is it?)

6. Definite articles are used with the names of some countries; however, all cities, countries, and continents require the definite article when they are modified: *El Brasil tiene música linda.* (Brazil has beautiful music.), *Soy de la Francia central.* (I'm from central France.)

---

7. Definite articles are used before the names of languages, except when the name follows the word *en* or the verb *hablar*: *El inglés es mi primer lenguaje.* (English is my first language.), *Todos hablan italiano.* (Everyone speaks Italian.)

8. Definite articles are never used after the verb *HABER*: *Hay moscas en la cocina.* (There are flies in the kitchen.) Nor is it used in compound nouns that are formed by the word *de*: *Nora tiene dolor de estómago.* (Nora has a stomachache.)

9. The definite article *el* is part of the only two contractions in Spanish, *al* (*a + el*) and *del* (*de + el*): *Vamos al parque.* (Let's go to the park.), *Es del doctor.* (It's from the doctor.)

---

10. Definite articles are used more frequently in Spanish than they are in English. Not only do they appear before specific persons, places, and things, but they are also used with nouns in a general, generic, or even abstract sense: *La leche tiene muchas vitaminas.* (Milk has a lot of vitamins.), *La vida es difícil.* (Life is tough.) Just don't use them before nouns that refer to an unspecified amount or incomplete set: *Necesitamos amor y cariño.* (We need love and care.)

¡SECRETOS!

Be careful! Some common phrases in English require the definite article in Spanish when translated:

Let's go home.	*Vamos a la casa.*
It's two dollars per pound.	*Cuesta dos dólares la libra.*
What's on T.V.?	*¿Que sale en la televisión?*

¿Quieres Practicar?

a.) Translate these phrases into English:

1. At seven o'clock   *A las siete.* _____

2. Lots of money   _____

3. On Thursday   _____

4. The boy and girl   _____

5. In Peru   _____

b.) Fill in the blank with the correct definite article:

1. __*la*__ *España*

2. _____ *inglés*

3. _____ *cervezas*

4. _____ *dentistas*

5. _____ *días*

5. *en el Perú*	5. *los*
4. *el niño y la niña*	4. *los*
3. *el jueves*	3. *las*
2. *mucho dinero*	2. *el*

¡OYE!

Why are they called "definite" articles? It's because *el* or *la* makes something "definite," clear, and specific. In contrast, the word *un* or *una* indicates one of many, "indefinite," or unspecific things. Notice:

Let's go to the party.   *Vamos a la fiesta.*

Let's go to a party.   *Vamos a una fiesta.*

II. Indefinite Article

There really isn't much else to learn about indefinite articles in Spanish, other than mentioning those situations where they need to be omitted:

1. The indefinite article is usually dropped after the verbs *tener, llevar, buscar, comprar, sacar,* and *usar*: *¿Tiene carro?* (Do you have a car?). In other words, think about the Spanish verb (action word) before you translate your articles into Spanish.

2. The indefinite article is also omitted before a simple predicate noun that indicates nationality, profession, religion, gender, rank, or marital status. Here are examples of a simple predicate noun: *Es <u>pintor</u>.* (He's a <u>painter</u>.), *Es <u>abuela</u>.* (She's a <u>grandmother</u>.), *Soy <u>cristiana</u>.* (I'm a <u>Christian</u>.)

3. The definite article is also omitted in many common expressions and exclamations, such as those with *¡Qué…!, mil, ciento, medio, otro, sin, tal,* and *cierto*: *¡Qué vista tan bonita!* (What a pretty view!), *en media hora* (in a half hour), *sin duda* (without a doubt).

Indefinite articles are everywhere in Spanish. Just be aware that the use or omission of an article can change the meaning of a sentence:

Ella no quiere agua. [She doesn't want (any) water.]
Ella no quiere <u>el</u> agua. [She doesn't want the water (that we know about).]
Ella no quiere <u>un</u> agua. [She doesn't want a (serving of) water.]

¡LEE Y ESCRIBE!

The singular masculine form *un* is used before all feminine nouns that begin with a stressed *á* or *ha*. The plural form of the article, however, is in the feminine:

Vi un águila.	I saw an eagle.
Vi unas águilas.	I saw a couple of eagles.
Tengo un hacha.	I have a hatchet.
Tengo unas hachas.	I have some hatchets.

¿Quieres Practicar?

Fill in each line with the appropriate indefinite article.

1. _____ *alma*   4. _____ *problemas*

2. _____ *agua*   5. _____ *irlandés*

3. _____ *lápices*

1. un   2. un   3. unos   4. unos   5. un

III. Neuter Article *Lo*

Lo is considered the neuter article in Spanish because it refers to neither the feminine nor the masculine. To get an "A+," learn the translation of each *lo* phrase below:

lo bueno	<u>*Lo* bueno</u>	*es que Carlos habla español.*
	The good thing	is that Carlos speaks Spanish.
lo difícil	<u>*Lo* difícil</u>	*es que él no habla inglés.*
	The difficult thing	is that he doesn't speak English.
lo bello	*Pensemos en*	<u>*lo* bello</u>.
	Let's think about	that which is beautiful.
lo nuevo	*¿Qué es*	<u>*lo* nuevo</u>?
	What is	the newest thing?

Check out these other *lo* expressions, which actually function by themselves:

Lo contrario	The opposite
Lo más posible	As much as possible
Lo único	The only one
Lo mismo	The same thing
Lo mejor	The best

¡CONVERSEMOS!

Although it sounds complicated, the Spanish construction *lo* + (ADJECTIVE or ADVERB) + *que* is a pretty common way to express "how" in English. Notice that the gender or number of the adjective does not matter—*lo* still stays the same:

Sabemos <u>lo inteligentes que</u> son.	We know how smart they are.
¿Vieron <u>lo caro que</u> fue?	Did you see how expensive it was?
Me dice <u>lo bien que</u> haces en la clase.	She tells me how well you're doing in class.

¿Quieres Practicar?

a.) Try to say the following aloud in Spanish:

1. what has been learned   *lo aprendido*

2. the good and the bad   _____

3. the most important thing   _____

4. the opposite   _____

5. what has been written   _____

b.) Explain the differences between the three main articles:
   DEFINITE, INDEFINITE, NEUTER

ADJECTIVES

There are only a few things to know about using adjectives in Spanish that will help to improve your grade:

I. Adjective Agreement

GENERAL RULES

Never forget that an adjective in Spanish must "agree" with the noun it modifies in gender and in number. Here's a typical example from a textbook:

delicious   MASCULINE   FEMININE

SINGULAR   *delicioso*   *deliciosa*

El taco es delicioso y la enchildada es deliciosa.

PLURAL   *deliciosos*   *deliciosas*

Los tacos son deliciosos y las enchildadas son deliciosas.

Generally in Spanish, whenever an adjective modifies, it is placed immediately after the noun:

Es un ta<u>co</u> delicio<u>so</u>.   *Son enchila<u>das</u> delicios<u>as</u>.*

Your turn:

Es un niño guap____ y son niñas bonit____.
It's a handsome boy and they are pretty girls.

Also remember that adjectives ending in a consonant (e.g., *social*) or *-e* (e.g., *grande*), have only ONE singular and ONE plural form: *social → sociales, grande → grandes.*

¡PALABRAS EXTRAS!

When talking in Spanish, tell yourself that the adjective <u>generally follows the noun</u>, even when it is modified by a little extra adverb:

No fue noche <u>tan</u> larga.	It wasn't that long of a night.
Tengo música <u>muy</u> linda.	I have very pretty music.
Quiere algo <u>más</u> dulce.	He wants something sweeter.

¿Quieres Practicar?

Change these words to plurals, but don't worry about translating them:

1. *inteligente*   _____

2. *lenta*   _____

3. *fácil*   _____

4. *hablador*   _____

5. *estudioso*   _____

1. *inteligentes*   2. *lentas*   3. *fáciles*   4. *habladores*   5. *estudiosos*

¡OYE!

When it comes to finding nationalities and/or places of origin in Spanish, just refer to a list of "Countries and Nationalities" either on the web or in a textbook.

II. Adjective Position

A. GENERAL RULES

Although adjectives in Spanish generally appear AFTER the nouns they modify, there are four main cases when they may be placed BEFORE.

1. Adjectives appear before the noun in exclamations with *Qué*:

¡Qué linda flor!	What a lovely flower!
¡Qué difícil problema!	What a difficult problem!

2. Adjectives of inherent nature or quality also precede the noun:

el frío hielo	the cold ice
el chistoso payaso	the funny clown

3. Adjectives go before a noun when they express a personal opinion or judgment:

Creo que tenemos el mejor carro.	I believe we have the best car.
Sin duda, esa fue mi peor clase.	Without a doubt, that was my worst class.

4. Adjectives that express number, limitation, or quantity also precede the noun:

Hemos tenido bastante ayuda.	We've had plenty of help.
No necesito tanto dinero.	I don't need that much money.

To learn these four cases where the adjective goes before the noun, simply memorize this line:

"¡Qué <u>frío viento</u>!", dijo el <u>feroz monstruo</u>. "<u>Buena idea</u> si salgo <u>otro día</u>."

"What a <u>cold wind</u>!" said the <u>ferocious monster</u>.
"<u>Good idea</u> if I go out <u>another day</u>."

1. *Qué* statement   2. Inherent quality   3. Opinion   4. Quantity

---

¡CONVERSEMOS!

Generally speaking, when an adjective follows a noun in Spanish, it often carries a more emphatic meaning than if it were placed before:

Fue un hermoso día.	It was a beautiful day.
¡Fue un día hermoso!	It was a beautiful day!

B. ADJECTIVES WITH SHORTENED FORMS

Some adjectives drop their final *o* when placed before a masculine noun, but they're easy to learn if you break them into sets of two or three. Notice the accent marks on *ningún* (not one) and *algún* (some):

uno	→	*un televisor*	(one TV)
primero	→	*primer hijo*	(first son)
bueno	→	*buen padre*	(good dad)
malo	→	*mal día*	(bad day)
alguno	→	*algún libro*	(some book)
ninguno	→	*ningún carro*	(not one car)

Here are the other two you'll need in order to get an A+ in Spanish:

1. *Grande* (big) becomes *gran* before a noun when it carries the meaning of "excellence" rather than size: *Tiene casa grande porque es gran persona.* (She's got a big house because she's a great person.)

2. *Ciento* (100) becomes *cien* only when it is directly followed by a masculine or feminine plural noun: *Hay cien niñas y cien niños aquí.* (There are one hundred girls and one hundred boys here.)

¡LEE Y ESCRIBE!

Santo (Saint) becomes *San* when it is followed by a proper noun not beginning with *To . . .* or *Do . . .*:

San José y San Francisco

Santa Ana y Santo Domingo

¿Quieres Practicar?

a.) Put the correct translation in order:

1. a very delicious pear   *deliciosa una muy pera*

2. the white snow   *blanca la nieve*

3. the green chairs   *sillas las verdes*

4. the other paper   *papel otro el*

5. What big eyes!   *grandes ojos Qué*

b.) Write the shortened forms of each adjective below along with its definition in English:

1. *tercero*   _tercer_   _third_

2. *grande*   _____   _____

3. *primero*   _____   _____

4. *alguno*   _____   _____

5. *bueno*   _____   _____

1. *una pera muy deliciosa*
2. *la blanca nieve*
3. *las sillas verdes*
4. *el otro papel*
5. *¡Qué grandes ojos!*

2. *gran* great
3. *primer* first
4. *algún* some
5. *buen* good

¡OYE!

Some adjectives actually differ in meaning depending on whether they precede or follow a noun:

el único carro
the only car

el carro único
the unique car

un buen estudiante
a fine student

un estudiante bueno
a well-behaved student

el gran actor
a great actor

el actor grande
the large actor

III. Other Uses of Adjectives

A. MORE THAN ONE ADJECTIVE

Only the top students know how adjectives are used in "special" situations. Notice the examples:

1. If nouns in a sentence are of different genders, the adjective that modifies them is generally left in the masculine plural: *Son hombres y mujeres europeos.* (They're European men and women.)

2. When two adjectives modify a noun, they are generally placed after it, joined by the word *y*: *Ella es una estudiante inteligente y disciplinada.* (She is an intelligent and disciplined student.)

3. However, the two adjectives may also be joined without the *y*, when the adjective of greater emphasis is mentioned last: *Tiene un sofá elegante <u>francés</u>.* (He's got an elegant French sofa.)

B. NOUNS USED AS ADJECTIVES

By the way, nouns in Spanish may be used as adjectives also: *Somos primos hermanos.* (We're first cousins.), but they don't have to agree in number and gender with the nouns they modify: *Son programas piloto.* (They are pilot programs.)

To sound more fluent, try to <u>use an adjective as a noun</u>! Simply replace the noun with the English equivalent of "the ___ one," or "the ___ person": *¿Quieres <u>el grande</u>?* (Do you want <u>the big one</u>?), *Tengo comida para <u>los pobres</u>.* (I have food for <u>the poor people</u>.)

¡PALABRAS EXTRAS!

Past participles can also be used as adjectives, but they must agree in both gender and number with the nouns they modify. You'll learn about past participles in chapter 6:

Hay dos sillas <u>pintadas</u>.   There are two painted chairs.

Mira el niño <u>mojado</u>.   Look at the wet child.

¿Quieres Practicar?

a.) Look up a translation of each adjective and place it <u>after</u> the noun or nouns:

1. UGLY	*mesas y sillas*	<u>*mesas y sillas feas*</u>
2. MODERN	*apartamentos y casas*	
3. RED & BLUE	*libros*	
4. NICE	*maestros y estudiantes*	
5. HAPPY	*muchachas y muchachos*	

b.) Create sentences that replace the noun with an article and adjective:

1. *Mira el carro sucio, blanco, etc.*   <u>*Mira el sucio.*</u>

2. *¿Dónde están las mesas negras, grandes, etc.?*

3. *Necesitamos la lámpara verde, bonita, etc.*

4. *No me gusta el libro azul, nuevo, etc.*

5. *Habla con los estudiantes cubanos, peruanos, etc.*

C. COMPARISON OF ADJECTIVES

Students often get confused when it comes to comparing things in Spanish, because they don't know which formula to use. These three will help when you compare adjectives:

1. *MÁS/MENOS _____ QUE*

   Jorge es más alto que su hermano. (Jorge is taller than his brother.), *Esta caja es menos cara que la otra.* (This box is less expensive than the other one.)

2. *BUENO → MEJOR, MALO → PEOR*

   La sopa es <u>mejor</u> que la ensalada. (The soup is <u>better</u> than the salad.), *El primer examen fue <u>peor</u> que el segundo.* (The first exam was <u>worse</u> than the second.)

3. *TAN + ADJECTIVE + COMO*

   Tus ojos son tan azules como el cielo. (Your eyes are as blue as the sky.), *Ellos hablan tan bien como Uds.* (They speak as well as you.)

D. OTHER WAYS TO SAY "THAN" IN SPANISH

Watch out how you translate "than" in Spanish! Here is where students make mistakes:

1. "Than" is translated by *de* before any number: *Es menos <u>de</u> 25 libras.* (It's less than 25 pounds.) NOT: *Es menos que 25 libras.*

2. "Than" is translated by *de* before phrases that take the place of a deleted noun, such as *el que, la que, los que,* and *las que,* which all mean "that or those which": *Recibimos más juguetes <u>de</u> los que nos regalaste.* (We received more toys than (the toys) you gave us.) NOT: *. . . más juguetes que los que . . .*

3. "Than" is translated by *de lo que* (than that which) whenever a clause suggests that there is already a standard for comparison established in a sentence: *La conversación fue más larga de lo que pensamos.* (The conversation was longer than what we thought.) NOT: *. . . más larga que lo que . . .*

 ## ¿Quieres Practicar?

Underline only those sentences that are grammatically correct:

1. *Él es mayor que su hermana.*

2. *Es más grande que lo que pensamos.*

3. *Son tan verdes como el mar.*

4. *Tengo menos que 40 años.*

5. *Hay más sillas de las que están en la otra clase.*

E. SUPERLATIVE ADJECTIVES

Superlatives tell which is the brightest, the biggest, and the best. Notice the order:

el gato	*más grande*	(the biggest cat)
noun	comparative form	

Now you translate one:

la pregunta	*más difícil*	_____

The pattern for comparing any two words in Spanish is pretty consistent. Stick with the *más que* pattern and you should be fine:

ADJECTIVES	*Es más <u>agudo</u> que una navaja.*
	It's sharper than a razor.
ADVERBS	*Pablo camina más <u>lentamente</u> que una tortuga.*
	He walks slower than a turtle.
NOUNS	*Ella tiene más <u>paciencia</u> que una santa.*
	She has more patience than a saint.
VERBS	*Ellos <u>trabajan</u> más que nosotros.*
	They work more than us.

¡LEE Y ESCRIBE!

If the adjective ends in a consonant or accented vowel, the suffix is simply added. In terms of spelling, the *z* changes to *c*, the *c* changes to *qu*, and the *g* changes to *gu* when *-ísimo* is added: *feliz → felicísimo; rico → riquísimo; largo → larguísimo.*

¿Quieres Practicar?

a.) Complete these sentences using *más que* or *mejor que*.

1. *los caballos son / fuerte / los pollos* <u>más fuertes que los pollos</u>

2. *los hijos son / viejo / los padres* _____

3. *El ratón es / grande / el elefante* _____

4. *La vida es / bueno / el dinero* _____

5. *Mickey Mouse es / famoso / tú* _____

b.) Fill in a description, change it to the superlative, and then translate to English:

1. *libro* _____   <u>el libro más nuevo</u>   <u>the newest book</u>

2. *hombres* _____   _____   _____

3. *oficinas* _____   _____   _____

4. *programa* _____   _____   _____

5. *perro* _____   _____   _____

5. *más famoso que tú*
4 *mejor que el dinero*
3. *más grande que el elefante*
2. *más viejos que los padres*

HOW TO GET AN A+

After reading this chapter on Spanish grammar, you should be able to name the principal parts of speech and explain the structure of a sentence, the use of nouns, and the use of descriptive adjectives. For sure, everything here is necessary if you want to get an A+ in Spanish. In the next chapter we'll continue our grammar study, as we prepare for the world of verbs. So be on the lookout. The fog will clear soon, everything will somehow come together, and all this Spanish grammar stuff will actually begin to make sense!

Chapter 5
Capítulo Cinco

Grammar—Part Two
La Gramática—Segunda Parte

DEMONSTRATIVES

I. Demonstrative Adjectives

Basically, demonstratives are words that point out or "demonstrate" something or someone. In English they are "this, that, these, and those." See how they refer to three different locations in Spanish:

THIS/ THESE (near the speaker)

	MASC.	FEM.	
SING.	*este*	*esta*	*Este libro es nuevo.* (This book is new.)
PL.	*estos*	*estas*	*Estos libros son nuevos.* (These books are new.)

THAT/ THOSE (near the person spoken to)

	MASC.	FEM.	
SING.	*ese*	*esa*	*Esa silla es grande.* (That chair is big.)
PL.	*esos*	*esas*	*Esas sillas son grandes.* (Those chairs are big.)

THAT/ THOSE (away from the speaker and the person spoken to)

	MASC.	FEM.	
SING.	*aquel*	*aquella*	*Aquel niño es alto.* (That boy there is tall.)
PL.	*aquellos*	*aquellas*	*Aquellos niños son altos.* (Those boys there are tall.)

To memorize these quickly, point to things around you while you practice each word!

¿Quieres Practicar?

Rewrite each sentence with the demonstrative adjective in the plural form:

1. *este hombre*   <u>estos hombres</u>

2. *esta silla*   _____

3. *aquel carro*   _____

4. *aquella montaña*   _____

5. *ese teléfono*   _____

5. *esos teléfonos*
4. *aquellas montañas*
3. *aquellos carros*
2. *estas sillas*

II. Demonstrative Pronouns

Demonstrative pronouns correspond to "this one," "that one," "these ones," and "those ones." In Spanish, demonstrative pronouns have the same forms as the adjectives but include accent marks over each stressed vowel:

THIS ONE/ THESE ONES (near the speaker)

	MASC.	FEM.	
SING.	*éste*	*ésta*	*Quiero ésta.* (I want <u>this</u> one.)
PL.	*éstos*	*éstas*	*Quiero éstas.* (I want <u>these</u> ones.)

THAT ONE/ THOSE ONES (near the person spoken to)

	MASC.	FEM.	
SING.	*ése*	*ésa*	*No quiero ése.* (I don't want <u>that</u> one.)
PL.	*ésos*	*ésas*	*No quiero ésos.* (I don't want <u>those</u> ones.)

THAT ONE/ THOSE ONES (away from the speaker and the person spoken to)

	MASC.	FEM.	
SING.	*aquél*	*aquélla*	*Necesito aquélla.* (I need <u>that</u> one over there.)
PL.	*aquéllos*	*aquéllas*	*Necesito aquéllas.* (I need <u>those</u> ones over there.)

¡CONVERSEMOS!

There are also three neuter demonstrative pronouns in Spanish—all ending in *-o* and without accent marks: *esto, eso,* and *aquello.* They are used in place of statements, concepts, ideas, or situations, and Spanish speakers use them all the time: *No entiendo esto.* (I don't understand this.), *Eso es todo.* (That's it.)

¿Quieres Practicar?

Change each English phrase to a demonstrative pronoun in Spanish:

1. this book   *éste*

2. that table way over there   _____

3. those ones   _____

4. these houses   _____

5. that child way over there   _____

2. aquélla   3. ésos   4. éstas   5. aquél

POSSESSIVES

I. Short-Form

These are called "short-form" possessives only because of their size. We won't even worry about the "long form" possessives because they are not used much. This chart is typical, and can be confusing unless you take the time to read it carefully:

SUBJECT PRONOUNS	POSSESSIVE ADJECTIVES	ENGLISH
Yo (I)	*mi/mis*	(my)
Tú (You)	*tu/tus*	(your: sing. inf.)
Él, Ella, Ud. (He, She, You)	*su/sus*	(his, her, its, their, your: sing. form.)
Nosotros/as (We)	*nuestro/nuestros* *nuestra/nuestras*	(our)
(***Vosotros/as***)*	***vuestro/vuestros*** ***vuestra/vuestras***	(your, pl. inf.)
Ellos/as, Uds. (They, You)	*su/sus*	(their, your: pl. form.)

****Vosotros***: This plural informal pronoun implies "you guys." It is used in Spain but very seldom in Latin America.

Look how the word *su* can mean "his, hers, its, their, or your" in Spanish. The language clarifies the problem by using the construction *de* + subject pronoun: *¿Qué necesita—el número de él o de ella?* [What do you need—his number (of he) or hers (of she)?].

 ### *¿Quieres Practicar?*

Show possession between the following sets of words and then translate if you like:

1. *El perro/ mi hermano*   *El perro de mi hermano* (My brother's dog)

2. *Los libros/ ellas*   _____

3. *El restaurante/ el hotel*   _____

4. *Las hijas/ Silvia*   _____

5. *El dinero/ tu familia*   _____

2. *Los libros de ellas*
3. *El restaurante del hotel*
4. *La hijas de Silvia*
5. *El dinero de tu familia*

¡OYE!

Speaking of possession, use *de* to ask "Whose?" in Spanish. It's used all the time with the connecting verb, *ser*:

¿De quién es el suéter?	Whose sweater is it?
¿De quién son estos formularios?	Whose forms are these?

PRONOUNS

Students can learn tips on how pronouns work once they divide them into types. We've aleady talked about demonstrative pronouns [i.e. *éste* (this one), *ésa* (that one)]. Here are the other types, along with suggestions on how to learn them.

I. Possessive Pronouns

A possessive pronoun not only expresses possession, but also takes the place of a noun. Possessive pronouns are formed by combining the definite article (*el, la, los, las*) with the long-form possessive adjective listed below: *Su libro es blanco y el mío es amarillo* (mine):

PRONOUN	MEANING
mío(s)/mía(s)	mine
tuyo(s)/tuya(s)	yours (inf.)
suyo(s)/suya(s)	his, hers, theirs, yours (form.)
nuestro(s)/nuestra(s)	ours

¡PALABRAS EXTRAS!

Do you recall the neuter pronoun *lo*? Notice the meanings of *lo mío, lo tuyo, lo suyo,* and *lo nuestro*:

Tengo lo mío.	I have mine.
No necesitas lo tuyo.	You don't need your stuff.
¿Qué pasó con lo suyo?	What happened to his part?
Lo nuestro está pagado.	Our portion is paid.

¿Quieres Practicar?

Replace the underlined words with a possessive pronoun:

1. *Ese carro es más grande que <u>nuestro carro</u>.*   el nuestro

2. *No tengo <u>mi computadora</u>.*

3. *¿Cuál es <u>su hijo</u>?*

4. *Ella respeta <u>las opiniones de Uds</u>.*

5. *Me gusta <u>tu bicicleta</u>.*

3. *el suyo*   5. *la tuya*
2. *la mía*   4. *las nuestras*

II. Personal Pronouns

A. SUBJECT PRONOUNS

Memorize these by "chanting" the pattern in these examples:

SINGULAR		PLURAL		EXAMPLES
yo	(I)	*nosotros/ as*	(we)	*<u>Yo</u> no, pero <u>nosotros</u> sí.*
tú	(<u>you</u>: sing. inf.)	*vosotros/ as*	(<u>you</u>: pl. inf.)	*<u>Tú</u> no, pero <u>vosotros</u> sí.*
él	(he)	*ellos*	(they, masc.)	*<u>Él</u> no, pero <u>ellos</u> sí.*
ella	(she)	*ellas*	(they, fem.)	*<u>Ella</u> no, pero <u>ellas</u> sí.*
Ud.	(<u>you</u>: sing. form.)	*Uds.*	(<u>you</u>: pl. form.)	*<u>Usted</u> no, pero <u>ustedes</u> sí.*

¡CONVERSEMOS!

Subject pronouns may be added for emphasis or to make the meaning clear:

Soy yo.	It is <u>I</u>.
Tú lo sabes.	<u>You</u> know it.
Habla mucho ella.	<u>She</u> talks a lot.

¡SECRETOS!

In Spain, the abbreviation for *usted (Ud.)* and *ustedes (Uds.)* is *Vd.* and *Vds. Usted* is known as the polite, respectful, or courteous form in Spanish, and it is often used to address those who are older or have a higher social status in society. It is also used when addressing new acquaintances or strangers. It is the way children are trained to address adults, and the way professionals address each other in businesses or at government offices.

In contrast, the familiar or informal *tú* form is generally used at home, on the job, in public, or at social gatherings when addressing friends, co-workers, relatives, and younger children. It is also the way one addresses a diety in prayer.

¿Quieres Practicar?

Replace the following words with the correct subject pronoun:

1. *Toda la clase y yo*   nosotros
2. *Sandra* _____
3. *Ud. y Alejandro* _____
4. *Mis amigas* _____
5. *Los maestros* _____

2. *ella*   3. *ustedes*   4. *ellas*   5. *ellos*

B. PREPOSITIONAL PRONOUNS

Spanish personal pronouns generally have the same form when used as objects of a preposition or as subjects of a verb. The only difference is that *mí* and *ti* replace *yo* and *tú* after most prepositions (i.e., *para, por, en, con,* etc.):

SINGULAR		PLURAL		EXAMPLES
mí	(me)	*nosotros/as*	(us)	*Es para mí.* (It's for me.)
ti	(you: sing. inf.)	*vosotros/as*	(you: pl. inf.)	*Es para ti.* (It's for you.)
él	(him)	*ellos*	(them, masc.)	
ella	(her)	*ellas*	(them, fem.)	
usted	(you: sing. form.)	*ustedes*	(you: pl. form.)	

Careful! When *mí* and *ti* are used as objects of the preposition *con*, they are joined together to form a single word: *con* + *mí* = <u>*conmigo*</u>: *¿Quieres hablar conmigo?* (Do you want to speak with me?); *con* + *ti* = <u>*contigo*</u>: *No quiero jugar contigo.* (I don't want to play with you.)

¡OYE!

In place of prepositional pronouns, however, the subject pronouns are used after the prepositions *según* (according to), *salvo, menos,* or *excepto* (except), *entre* (between), and *como* (like):

Mi hijo habla como yo.   My son talks like me.
Todos trabajan menos tú.   Everyone works except you.
No hay nada entre tú y yo.   There is nothing between you and me.

¿Quieres Practicar?

Insert your choice of pronouns to complete each sentence:

1. *Las cápsulas son para _____.*   ____ella____

2. *Su oficina está enfrente de _____.*   _____

3. *El carro es para _____.*   _____

4. *Tienen confianza en _____.*   _____

5. *No vive con _____.*   _____

C. DIRECT OBJECT PRONOUNS (THE *LO-LA* WORDS)

When you were learning about sentences in Spanish, you saw that a direct object (D.O.) noun receives the action of the verb directly. Well, there are personal pronouns called direct object pronouns that do the same thing. They do it by taking the place of the direct object noun so it doesn't have to be repeated: *Pego la pelota.* (I hit the ball.) → *La pego.* (I hit it.) Here's the full chart:

SINGULAR	D.O. PRONOUNS	PLURAL	D.O. PRONOUNS
yo	*me*	*nosotros*	*nos*
tú	*te*	*vosotros*	*os*
él	*lo*	*ellos*	*los*
ella	*la*	*ellas*	*las*
Ud.	*lo/ la*	*Uds.*	*los/las*

The *Ud./Uds.* forms can be either masc. or fem., depending on who you're talking about. Also observe how <u>these pronouns usually precede the verb form</u>, which is the opposite of English:

No <u>los</u> veo.   I don't see <u>them</u>.
Nosotros <u>la</u> visitamos.   We visited <u>her</u>.

Attention A+ students! Direct object pronouns are also found in other places in Spanish. To learn these other key positions, practice the following SAMPLE sentences, instead of memorizing all the grammatical terminology:

1. Attach the D.O. pronouns after an IMPERATIVE and before it in the negative.

   SAMPLE: *Tráigalas y no las traiga.* (Bring <u>them</u> and don't bring <u>them</u>.)

2. Attach the D.O. pronouns after the *ESTAR* + PRESENT PARTICIPLE construction and before it in the negative.

   SAMPLE: *Estoy leyéndolo y no lo estoy leyendo.* (I'm reading <u>it</u> and I'm not reading <u>it</u>.)

3. Attach the D.O. pronouns after the VERB + INFINITIVE construction and before it in the negative.

   SAMPLE: *Puede besarme y no me puede besar.* (She can kiss <u>me</u> and she can't kiss <u>me</u>.)

Obviously, the *lo, la, los,* or *las* can get confusing in a sentence. For example, *La encontré* can mean "I found you (f.), or her, or it (f.)." To clarify, simply add prepositional pronouns using *a* before a name or subject pronoun:

La encontré <u>a ella</u>.	I found her.
La encontré <u>a María</u>.	I found María.
La encontré <u>a Ud</u>.	I found you (a female).

¿Quieres Practicar?

a.) Change the underlined noun to a direct object pronoun and place it in a new sentence:

1. *Tengo <u>el mapa</u>.* <u>*Lo* tengo.</u>

2. *No veo <u>a Uds</u>.* (m.) *No _____ veo.*

3. *Estoy estudiando <u>la lección</u>. _____ estoy estudiando./Estoy estudiando___.*

4. *No visita a <u>nosotros</u>. No _____ visita.*

5. *Están buscando a <u>Felipe</u>. _____ están buscando./Están buscando___.*

b.) Change these negative commands to the affirmative:

1. *No lo traiga.* <u>   Tráigalo.   </u>   4. *No la apague.* _____

2. *No me enseñe.* _____   5. *No nos invite.* _____

3. *No los toque.* _____

3. *La/la*	5. *Lo/lo*	3. *Tóquelos*	5. *Invítenos*
2. *los*	4. *nos*	2. *Enséñeme*	4. *Apáguela*

D. INDIRECT OBJECT PRONOUNS (*ME, TE, LE, NOS, OS, LES*)

Indirect object pronouns generally refer to people, showing to whom or for whom the action of a verb is completed. Like all object pronouns, these words cannot stand alone and usually precede the conjugated verb in a sentence: *Me habla.* (He speaks to me.). Compare this chart with the previous one:

SINGULAR		PLURAL	
yo	*me*	*nosotros*	*nos*
tú	*te*	*vosotros*	*os*
él, ella, Ud.	*le*	*ellos, ellas, Uds.*	*les*

An indirect object (I.O.) receives the action of the verb indirectly, either through the direct object or by being affected in some other way by the verb:

I.O.	VERB	D.O.	
Te	*mando*	*la información.*	I'll send you the information.
Me	*dice*	*la verdad.*	She tells me the truth.
Le	*piden*	*su licencia.*	They ask for his license.

Good news! I.O. pronouns have the same main positions in a sentence as D.O. pronouns:

1. *Enséñeme y no me enseñe.* (Show to me and don't show to me.)
2. *Estoy dándole y no le estoy dando.* (I'm giving to him and I'm not giving to him.)
3. *Puede decirles y no les puede decir.* (She can say to them and she can't say to them.)

And since *le* and *les* can mean different things, clarify by adding *a* before a person, group, or prepositional pronoun. This phrase is generally placed at the beginning of the sentence: *A los niños siempre les compra zapatos nuevos.* [(to the boys) She always buys them new shoes.]

¡PALABRAS EXTRAS!

Several verbs in Spanish are used regularly with an indirect object pronoun. In the sentence, a thing (the direct object) is usually given to or taken from a person (the indirect object pronoun):

mandar	to send
mandarle algo a alguien	to send something to someone
Le mandaron la bicicleta (a él).	They sent him the bike.
robar	to steal
robarle algo a alguien	to steal something from someone
Me ha robado el saco (a mí).	She's stolen my sportscoat from me.

¿Quieres Practicar?

Exchange the underlined pronoun with another one. Then translate your new sentence:

1. *Ella <u>me</u> da muchas flores.*   <u>*Ella les da muchas flores.*</u>
   (She gives them many flowers.)

2. *¿<u>Nos</u> manda los datos?*   _____

3. *<u>Le</u> dijo todos los números.*   _____

4. *Está enseñánd<u>ole</u>s arte.*   _____

5. *<u>Le</u> mostraron el caballo.*   _____

So what's the easiest way to remember the difference between the <u>D.O. pronoun</u> and the <u>I.O. pronoun</u> in Spanish? No problem! The D.O. answers the question "what?" or "whom?" with regard to what the subject of the sentence is doing, while the I.O. tells where the D.O. is going.

E. DOUBLE OBJECT PRONOUNS

This is pretty straightforward. When a verb in Spanish has two pronoun objects, <u>the indirect object precedes the direct object</u>. And they both are placed <u>before</u> the verb:

Ella	*me*	*las*	*mandó.* (She sent them to me.)
	I.O. PRONOUN	D.O. PRONOUN	VERB

Ellos	*te*	*lo*	*explican.* (They explain it to you.)
	I.O. PRONOUN	D.O. PRONOUN	VERB

But, here's where Spanish students panic: If the two pronouns are in the third person—where the indirect object pronoun *le* or *les* precedes the direct object pronoun *lo, la, los,* or *las*—then the indirect object changes to the word *se*:

Él (le) lo dijo.	→	*Él se lo dijo.*	He told it to her.
Ella (les) la prestó.	→	*Ella se la prestó.*	She loaned it to them.

Since it has several meanings, *se* can obviously create confusion in a sentence if the context is unclear. To clarify, add the familiar *A* + PREPOSITIONAL PRONOUN construction:

Se los explicamos <u>a él</u>.	We explained them <u>to him</u>.
No se la traigo <u>a ellas</u>.	I don't bring it <u>to them</u>.
¿Se lo dan <u>a Ud.</u>?	Do they give it <u>to you</u>?

To get an A+ on a double object pronoun quiz, just focus on these three simple rules:

1. I.O. BEFORE D.O. AND THEY CAN'T BE SPLIT IN A SENTENCE!
2. NO TWO *L* WORDS IN A ROW!
3. CLARIFY *SE* WITH *A* + PREPOSITIONAL PRONOUN!

¡LEE Y ESCRIBE!

Direct object pronouns are positioned in a sentence the same as direct or indirect object pronouns. Just watch out for the accent mark that is placed over the stressed vowel:

Están enseñándomela.	They're teaching it to me.
¿Podrías mandárselos?	Could you send them to her?
Dígaselo a Francisco.	Tell it to Francisco.

¿Quieres Practicar?

Rewrite each sentence to include a double object pronoun:

1. *Le venden los tacos a Guadalupe.* (le + los) <u>Se los venden.</u>

2. *Les doy el dinero a él.* (les + lo) _____

3. *Le compra computadoras a la escuela.* (le + las) _____

4. *Le mandamos la mesa al maestro.* (le + la) _____

5. *Les traigo las revistas a Uds.* (les + las) _____

2. *Se lo doy* 3. *Se las compra*
4. *Se la mandamos* 5. *Se las traigo*

¡CONVERSEMOS!

There are also reflexive pronouns in Spanish, which we'll learn about when we study reflexive verbs in Chapter 7. Reflexive pronouns are used in both Spanish and English whenever the subject of a verb is also its object. In other words, reflexive pronouns are used when the subject of a sentence is acting on itself. An example is the *me* in *me veo* ("myself" in "I see myself"), where the person seeing and the person seen are one and the same.

III. Relative Pronouns: The "that" Words

A relative pronoun is used to combine or "relate" two sentences that refer to the same noun:

SINGULAR FORMS		PLURAL FORMS	
MASCULINE	FEMININE	MASCULINE	FEMININE
que	*que*	*que*	*que*
quien	*quien*	*quienes*	*quienes*
el que	*la que*	*los que*	*las que*
el cual	*la cual*	*los cuales*	*las cuales*
cuyo	*cuya*	*cuyos*	*cuyas*
cuanto	*cuanta*	*cuantos*	*cuantas*

A. RELATIVE PRONOUN *QUE*

Review this example of a relative pronoun with *que* (that, who, whom, or which), which is used for just about everything. Follow the three-step process:

1. Take two related sentences:　　*El carro cuesta mucho. El carro va rápido.*
　　　　　　　　　　　　　　　　The car costs a lot. The car goes fast.
2. Replace the noun in the second sentence with the relative pronoun (*que*).
3. Insert the new relative clause (which begins with the relative pronoun):

MAIN CLAUSE　　　　　　　RELATIVE CLAUSE
El carro cuesta mucho.　　+　　*que va rápido.*
　　　=　*El carro que va rápido cuesta mucho.*
　　　　The car that goes fast costs a lot.

Now, you try to combine these two sentences using the relative pronoun *que*:

Los papeles son importantes. Los papeles están en la oficina.
The papers are important. The papers are in the office.

_____

The papers that are in the office are important.

Check out these other uses of *que*. Remember it's not affected by gender or number:

El hombre que respeto es el director.
The man (whom) I respect is the principal.

Aquellos que ganan son felices.
Those (who) win are happy.

Tráigame los clavos que están en el garaje.
Bring me the nails (that) are in the garage.

¿Quieres Practicar?

Use *que* to combine each pair of sentences below. You have two choices:

1. *El postre tiene chocolate. El postre es blanco.*

   El postre que es blanco tiene chocolate.
   _____

2. *La señora vive en la ciudad. La señora tiene caballos.*

   _____

3. *La clase es buena. La clase dura tres horas.*

   _____

4. *Los estudiantes son italianos. Los estudiantes hablan inglés.*

   _____

5. *Las sillas están en la clase. Las sillas son negras.*

   _____

B. RELATIVE PRONOUN *QUIEN*

The relative pronoun *quien* or *quienes* refers only to people and identifies the noun more clearly than *que*. It is often used after the preposition *a* and agrees in number with the noun. Notice how *a quien* and *a quienes* can replace *que* when the noun is the direct object of the verb in the clause:

Ves a los niños. Los niños son amigos.
You see the boys. The boys are friends.
Los niños <u>a quienes</u> ves son amigos.
The boys <u>whom</u> you see are friends.

Doy comida a ese hombre. Ese hombre vive en el parque.
I give food to that man. That man lives in the park.
Ese hombre <u>a quien</u> doy comida vive en el parque.
That man <u>who</u> I give food to lives in the park.

¿Quieres Practicar?

Try to translate the underlined sentences the best way possible:

1. *Ya salieron los niños. Los vimos en el mercado ayer.*
   (The kids already left. We saw them at the market yesterday.)

   <u>*Ya salieron los niños a quienes vimos en el mercado ayer.*</u>

2. *El chofer llegó temprano. Lo llamamos a las ocho.*
   (The driver arrived early. We called him at eight o'clock.)

   <u>*El chofer a quien llamamos a las ocho llegó temprano.*</u>

3. *La chica siempre está enferma. La conocí el año pasado.*
   (The girl is always sick. I met her last year.)

   <u>*La chica a quien conocí el año pasado está enferma.*</u>

C. RELATIVE PRONOUNS *EL QUE* AND *EL CUAL*

These can be a pain for students, so pay attention: *el que, los que, la que, las que, el cual, los cuales, la cual,* and *las cuales* may be used in place of *que* or *a quien* when the relative pronoun is the object of the verb and the primary noun is a person. Notice the personal *a*:

La supervisora a <u>la que</u> llamamos se llama Celia.
The supervisor to (whom) we called is named Celia.
We called <u>whom</u> (obj.)? <u>Celia</u>!

Las enfermeras a <u>las que</u> conozco trabajan mañana.
The nurses of (whom) I know work tomorrow.
I know <u>who</u> (obj.)? <u>The nurses</u>!

By the way, *lo que* and *lo cual* appear in clauses, set apart by commas, which refer to a preceding concept or clause:

Alma practica su fe todos los días, lo que respeto mucho de ella.
Alma practices her faith every day, (which) I respect her a great deal for.

Donamos toda la ropa usada, lo cual yo espero que Uds. hagan también.
We donated all of the used clothing, (which) I hope you guys do as well.

¿Quieres Practicar?

Insert the correct relative pronoun into each sentence below:

1. *El doctor, _____ trabaja en Chicago, vive en Miami.*
2. *Nunca conversan, _____ sorprende a todos.*
3. *Esos hombres, _____ hablan español, son los maestros.*
4. *La estudiante, _____ está en frente de la clase, es mi prima.*
5. *Todas tus amigas, _____ bailan bien, van a la fiesta.*

A. *la que*
B. *el que*
C. *las que*
D. *lo que*
E. *los que*

1. B.   2. D.
3. E.   4. A.
5. C.

D. RELATIVE PRONOUNS AFTER PREPOSITIONS

Prepositions such as *con, de, a, en,* and *por* are often followed by relative pronouns. The rules change slightly depending on whether you refer to people or things:

El muchacho <u>con quien</u>   *sale ya tiene una novia.*
The boy (with whom)   she goes out already has a girlfriend.

El carro <u>en el cual</u>   *van a las conferencias es un convertible.*
The car (in which)   they go to the conferences is a convertible.

La libertad <u>por la que</u> luchamos es preciosa.
The liberty (for which) we fight is precious.

No he visto la película <u>de que</u> me hablaste.
I have not seen the film (that) you talked to me about.

¿Quieres Practicar?

Create sentences that refer to the following relative pronouns:

1. *que* _____

2. *la cual* _____

3. *quienes* _____

4. *el que* _____

5. *las que* _____

¡OYE!

Most of the time, *lo que* is simply used to mean "what." It's a great way to make a general statement:

No entiendo <u>lo que</u> dice.   I don't understand <u>what</u> he's saying.

<u>Lo que</u> me gusta es la comida.   <u>What</u> I like is the food.

Be sure you review this chart of personal pronouns as often as you can, because using these correctly will give you a great shot at getting that A+ in Spanish.

Personal Pronouns			
Subject	Indirect Object	Direct Object	Object of Preposition
yo	*me*	*me*	*mí*
tú	*te*	*te*	*ti*
Ud.		*lo, la*	*Ud.*
él	*le*	*lo*	*él*
ella		*la*	*ella*
nosotros, -as	*nos*	*nos*	*nosotros, -as*
vosotros, -as	*os*	*os*	*vosotros, -as*
ustedes [Uds.]		*los, las*	*ustedes*
ellos	*les*	*los*	*ellos*
ellas		*las*	*ellas*
= I, you, he, she, it, we, you, they	= to me, to you, to him, to her, to it, to us, to you, to them	= me, you, him, her, it, us, you, them	= [e.g., from] me, you, him, her, it, us, you, them

> Bear in mind that to get an A+ in Spanish, you'll need to master
> the more difficult parts of the language first!

PREPOSITIONS

Here's a great list of prepositions in Spanish, some of which you have seen before. These include some time and location words:

a	to, at, by means of	*La familia va a Florida.*
antes de	before	*Estudio antes del examen.*
bajo	under	*Mi suéter está bajo la silla.*
cerca de	near	*El niño está cerca de su mamá.*
con	with	*Lupe está con el perro.*
de	of, from, implies possession	*El profesor es de Argentina.*
debajo de	underneath	*Los zapatos están debajo de la cama.*
dentro de	inside	*El dinero está dentro del banco.*
después de	after	*Trabajo después de la clase.*
detrás de	behind	*Victor está detrás de Susana.*
durante	during	*¿Qué pasó durante la clase?*
en	in, on, at	*El restaurante está en el hotel.*
encima de	on top of	*El hombre trabaja encima del techo.*
enfrente de	in front of	*Las plantas están enfrente de la oficina.*
fuera de	outside of	*El agua va fuera de aquí.*
lejos de	far from	*Vivimos lejos de la ciudad.*
para	in order to, for	*La ensalada es para usted.*
por	by, through, for	*Vamos por el corredor.*
sin	without	*No estudio sin libro de texto.*
sobre	over, about	*Hay muchos papeles sobre la mesa.*

¡PALABRAS EXTRAS!

The preposition *sobre* has several different meanings in English:

Siempre discuten sobre la política.	They always argue about politics.
Va a llegar ella sobre las ocho.	She'll arrive approximately at eight.
Las nubes pasan sobre el valle.	The clouds pass over the valley.

Many prepositions include the little preposition *de*:

al lado de	beside	*a lo largo de*	along
alrededor de	around	*a través de*	through

¿*Quieres Practicar?*

Write in a preposition that has an opposite meaning:

1. *con* _____

2. *detrás de* _____

3. *bajo de* _____

4. *antes* _____

5. *dentro de* _____

1. *sin*   2. *enfrente de*   3. *arriba de*   4. *después*   5. *fuera de*

I. Using the Preposition *de*

The preposition *de* can be used in "Super Seven" ways:

1. <u>Description</u>:
   Mario es el hombre de pelo largo. Mario is the long-haired man. (man <u>of</u> long hair)

2. <u>Possession</u>:
   ¿Cuál es la capital de California? What's the capital <u>of</u> California?

3. <u>Origin</u>:
   Somos de México. We're <u>from</u> Mexico.

4. <u>Composition</u>:
   Tengo un collar de plata. I have a silver necklace. (necklace <u>of</u> silver)

5. <u>Content</u>:
   Traiga la caja de libros. Bring the box <u>of</u> books.

6. <u>Movement</u>:
   Están saliendo de la casa. They are leaving the house. (leaving <u>from</u>)

7. <u>Cause</u>:
   Sufren de sed. They suffer <u>from</u> thirst.

¡OYE!

Don't forget that *de* is also used with verbs:

Acabo de llamar.	I just called.
Favor de firmar.	Please sign.
Se olvida de todo.	He forgets everything.
Me acuerdo de ti.	I remember you.
Me acuerdo de ella.	I remember her.

¿Quieres Practicar?

Translate these phrases and sentences into English:

1. *la ensalada de fruta* _____

2. *dos de la mañana* _____

3. *el apartamento de Carlos* _____

4. *De nada.* _____

5. *¿De dónde es Ud.?* _____

3. Carlos's apartment
2. two in the morning
1. fruit salad

5. Where are you from?
4. You're welcome.

II. Using the Preposition *a*

The preposition *a* causes trouble, because it also has various translations in Spanish. To simplify, let's concentrate on the two main ways it can be used:

1. MOTION: Many times, the preposition *a* implies motion "to" somewhere: *Voy a la clase.* (I go to class.) It may also link a verb of motion "to" an infinitive, or base verb: *Salgo a comer.* (I go out to eat.) It even implies motion "to" someone when you use it with indirect object pronouns: *Le hablo a Carlos.* (I speak to Carlos.)

2. PERSONAL: The preposition *a* is also frequently used as a personal *a* before direct objects that refer to people or personified things: *Invitamos a tu hermano.* (We're inviting your brother.)

First focus on how *a* in Spanish refers to MOTION and PERSONAL, and then take care of these other common uses:

1. <u>How something is done</u>: *a la italiana* (Italian style), *a pie* (on foot)

2. <u>A price, rate, or pace</u>: *a diez millas por hora* (10 mph), *a la semana* (per week)

3. <u>At, upon, on</u>: *a la una* (at 1:00), *al entrar* (upon entering), *a la derecha* (on the right)

4. <u>Distance or time period</u>: *a una milla* (a mile away), *a los cinco años* (for five years)

5. <u>Everyday words and phrases</u>: *a veces* (sometimes), *a ver* (let's see), *a menudo* (often)

¿Quieres Practicar?

Translate these sentences into English:

1. *Ayudamos a los amigos.*   <u>We helped our friends.</u>
2. *Llamamos al doctor.*   _____
3. *Vamos a la playa.*   _____
4. *No visitamos a nadie.*   _____
5. *¿Le invitamos a Rafael?*   _____
6. *Trabajamos a los dos.*   _____
7. *Le operamos al paciente.*   _____
8. *Lo preparamos a mano.*   _____
9. *Escribimos a la familia.*   _____
10. *No le hablamos a ella.*   _____

2. We called the doctor.
3. Let's go to the beach.
4. We don't visit anyone.
5. Did we invite Rafael?
6. We work at two.
7. We operated on the patient.
8. We prepared it by hand.
9. We wrote to the family.
10. We didn't talk to her.

III. Using the Preposition *con*

The preposition *con* generally means "with" in English and can imply a variety of things, including <u>accompaniment</u>, <u>possession</u>, <u>description</u>, <u>method</u>, or <u>relationship</u>:

1. *Trabajan con mis amigos.* (They work <u>with</u> my friends.)
2. *Ordenamos más frijoles con arroz.* (We order more beans <u>with</u> rice.)
3. *¿Dónde vive la señora con los gatos?* (Where does the lady <u>with</u> the cats live?)
4. *Llama al chico con el pelo largo.* (Call the boy <u>with</u> the long hair.)
5. *No vive ella con su padre.* (She doesn't live <u>with</u> her father.)
6. *Lavamos los carros con mucho agua.* (We wash cars <u>with</u> lots of water.)
7. *Cuidamos a los niños con amor.* (We care for the children <u>with</u> love.)

¡LEE Y ESCRIBE!

Sometimes you'll see the preposition *con* linked to a pronoun, as in *con* + *mí* = *conmigo* (with me) or *con* + *tí* = *contigo* (with you).

¿Quieres Practicar?

Translate these phrases into English:

1. *Estamos contigo*   <u>We're with you.</u>

2. *Estamos con computadoras*

3. *Estamos con su esposa*

4. *Estamos con pelo largo*

5. *Estamos con amor*

6. *Estamos con prisa*

7. *Estamos con tráfico*

8. *Estamos con timidez*

9. *Estamos con zapatos negros*

10. *Estamos con hambre*

2. We have computers.
3. We're with his wife.
4. We have long hair.
5. We're in love.
6. We're in a hurry.
7. We're caught in traffic.
8. We're shy.
9. We're wearing black shoes.
10. We're hungry.

IV. Using the Preposition *en*

The preposition *en* usually means "in," "into," "on," "upon," or "at" in Spanish and indicates LOCATION or TIME: *Mi libro está en la cocina.* (My book is in the kitchen.), *No estudiamos en el verano.* (We don't study in the summer.) Sometimes, the preposition *en* can express "how" something is done: *Viajamos en metro o en autobús.* [We travel by (on a) subway or by (in a) bus.]

Where it gets strange is when *en* becomes part of Spanish verb infinitives or common expressions. They have to be memorized because the meaning of *en* is not very clear:

fijarse en	to notice	*en cambio*	on the other hand
pensar en	to think of	*en serio*	seriously
convertirse en	to turn into	*en seguida*	right away

The secret is to keep it simple, especially if you need to come up with Spanish on your own, by thinking of *en* as the word for "in," "on," or "at." You can work on the other translations and uses of the preposition *en* later.

¿Quieres Practicar?

Read the English phrase and then create a complete sentence using the preposition *en*:

1. in ten minutes   *Voy en diez minutos.*

2. in the kitchen

3. at the table

4. on the chair

5. in a day

V. Using the Prepositions *Para* and *Por*

Para and *por* generally mean "for" in Spanish, but they are used differently. The trouble is you won't get an A+ in Spanish if you constantly mix them up! Remember that *por* usually focuses <u>back</u> on a cause, while *para* generally refers <u>forward</u> to a result. Look at each sample below, fill in the blank, and then come up with a sentence on your own:

PARA (for, in order to)

They will leave for France.   *Saldrán para Francia.*

for Chicago   **Saldrán para Chicago.**

The chair is for you.   *La silla es para Ud.*

it's for María

I'll take a taxi downtown.   *Tomaré un taxi para el centro.*

a taxi home

The glass is for the water.   *El vaso es para el agua.*

it's for the wine

This is for the car.   *Este es para el carro.*

for the class

It's not for washing.   *No es para lavar.*

for cooking

She's here to help you.   *Está aquí para ayudarte.*

to visit you

I'm studying to be a doctor.   *Estudio para ser médico.*

to be a teacher

We have a date for Tuesday.   *Tenemos cita para el martes.*

a date for tomorrow

It's twenty until five.   *Son veinte para las cinco.*

ten until ten

To me, the price is OK.   *Para mí, el precio está bien.*

To her,

POR (for, by, through, in exchange for)

I travel by train.   *Viajo por tren.*

by car

I worked in place of her.   *Trabajé por ella.*

in place of Rosa

How much was the book?   *¿Cuánto pagó por el libro?*

for the table?

It was due to the wind.   *Era por el viento.*

due to the cold

I ran through the park.   *Corría por el parque.*

through the house

There was a tree near there.   *Había un árbol por allí.*

around here

I've painted for years.   *He pintado por años.*

for days

He came at night.   *Vino por la noche.*

in the afternoon

It went 80 mph.   *Andaba a ochenta millas por hora.*

50 mph

Two times two is four.   *Dos por dos son cuatro.*

five times five

It was written by Cervantes.	*Fue escrito por Cervantes.*
written by Prada	
He was about to leave.	*Estaba por salir.*
about to eat	
We heard it on the news.	*Lo escuchamos por las noticias.*
on the radio	

 ## *¿Quieres Practicar?*

Fill in the blanks with either PARA or POR. Remind yourself that *por* usually focuses <u>back</u> on a cause, while *para* generally refers <u>forward</u> to a result:

1. *Son producidos <u>por</u> máquinas.*   They're produced by machines.

2. *Nanita viene _____ ayudarnos.*   Nanita is coming to help us.

3. *¿ _____ qué es el martillo?*   What is the hammer for?

4. *Iris trabaja _____ Hortencia.*   Iris works in place of Hortencia.

5. *No puedes salir _____ esa puerta.*   You can't leave through that door.

6. *Hay una escuela _____ aquí.*   There's a school around here.

7. *Se venden _____ libra.*   They're sold by the pound.

8. *Tengo cita _____ mañana.*   I have an appointment for tomorrow.

9. *Ha vivido aquí _____ dos días.*   He's lived here for two days.

10. *Necesito dinero _____ este viaje.*   I need money for this trip.

4. *por*	7. *por*	10. *para*
3. *para*	6. *por*	9. *por*
2. *para*	5. *por*	8. *para*

ADVERBS

An adverb in a sentence answers a variety of questions such as "how" (adverbs of manner), "when" (adverbs of time), "where" (adverbs of place), and "how much" (adverbs of quantity). In English, many adverbs end with the letters "-ly." In Spanish, most are formed by adding *-mente* to the feminine form of an adjective (descriptive word):

ADJECTIVE (f.)		ADVERB	
correcta	correct	*correctamente*	correctly
lenta	slow	*lentamente*	slowly
clara	clear	*claramente*	clearly
cómoda	comfortable	*cómodamente*	comfortably
distinta	distinct	*distintamente*	distinctly
intensa	intense	*intensamente*	intensely
cuidadosa	careful	*cuidadosamente*	carefully
rápida	quick	*rápidamente*	quickly

To those adjectives with no specific feminine form, *-mente* is just added to the word:

ADJECTIVE		ADVERB	
final	final	*finalmente*	finally
feliz	happy	*felizmente*	happily
probable	probable	*probablemente*	probably

Bear in mind a few adverbs have irregular forms, without any *-mente* suffix. Note how some of these can also work as adjectives that describe nouns:

bien	*Ella canta bien.*	She sings well.
mal	*Pronuncio la letra mal.*	I pronounce the letter poorly.
mejor	*¿Está caminando mejor?*	Is he walking better?
peor	*Hablan peor que nosotros.*	They speak worse than us.
tanto	*Te quiero tanto.*	I love you so much.
mucho	*Escribimos mucho.*	We write a lot.
poco	*Hace muy poco.*	He does very little.

I. Adverbs of Manner

In your textbook, most adverbs are called adverbs of manner because they tell how something is done:

Hablamos <u>honestamente</u>. (We speak honestly.)
Examinan a los pacientes <u>físicamente</u>. (They physically examine the patients.)

And when two or more adverbs ending in *-mente* modify the same word, the suffix is added to the last adverb only. All the others remain in their singular form:

Los soldados están trabajando valiente y profesionalmente.
The soldiers are working bravely and professionally.

¡CONVERSEMOS!

Adverbs that modify other adverbs (or adjectives) are placed <u>before</u> the words they modify, which makes sense when you're talking to someone. It's just like English:

Estamos <u>totalmente</u> perdidos.   We are totally lost.

Vuelan <u>muy</u> lentamente.   They fly very slowly.

Piense <u>menos</u> negativamente.   Think less negatively.

¿Quieres Practicar?

Change these adjectives to their adverbial form:

1. verbal   <u>verbalmente</u>   6. científico   _____

2. inteligente   _____   7. verdadero   _____

3. histórico   _____   8. triste   _____

4. natural   _____   9. abierto   _____

5. simple   _____   10. desafortunado   _____

2. inteligentemente
3. históricamente
4. naturalmente
5. simplemente
6. científicamente
7. verdaderamente
8. tristemente
9. abiertamente
10. desafortunadamente

¡OYE!

Spanish adverbs are used in comparisons much like adjectives:

Virginia maneja menos cuidadosamente que Miguel.
Virginia drives less carefully than Miguel.

Sally corre más rapidamente que los otros.
Sally runs faster than the others.

II. Adverbs of Time

In Spanish, adverbs of time are found just about anywhere in a sentence. They answer the question, *¿Cuándo?* (When?):

Siempre voy al parque.	I always go to the park.
Ahora son las dos.	It's two o'clock now.
Comió durante la fiesta.	He ate during the party.
Bailaba mientras conversabas.	I danced while you talked.
Fuimos anteayer.	We went the day before yesterday.
Estudiarán luego.	They'll study later.

¿Quieres Practicar?

Translate these sentences into Spanish:

1. He already speaks Spanish.   *Ya habla español.*

2. He never speaks Spanish.   _____

3. He generally speaks Spanish.   _____

4. He speaks Spanish every day.   _____

5. He always speaks Spanish.   _____

5. *Siempre habla Español.*
4. *Todos los días habla Español.*
3. *Generalmente habla Español.*
2. *Nunca habla Español.*

III. Adverbs of Location

There are also several common adverbs of location or place in Spanish that answer the question, "Where?":

en	in, on, at	*fuera de*	outside of
encima de	on top of	*lejos de*	far from
enfrente de	in front of		

See how many combine with prepositions and other adverbs to create longer adverbial phrases:

hasta aquí	up to here	*a lo largo de*	along
desde allí	from there	*al lado de*	beside
al fondo	at the bottom		

¿Quieres Practicar?

Write the opposite of each word or phrase:

1. *delante* <u> *detrás* </u>   4. *a la izquierda* _____

2. *lejos* _____   5. *arriba* _____

3. *adentro* _____

2. *cerca*   3. *afuera*

4. *a la derecha*   5. *abajo*

> **¡PALABRAS EXTRAS!**
>
> Some Spanish programs teach you about two other kinds of adverbs, but we'll refer to them as essential vocabulary:
>
> Adverbs of affirmation [i.e., *sí* (yes)]
>
> Adverbs of negation [i.e., *nunca* (never), *nada* (nothing)]

IV. Adverbs of Quantity

These adverbs tell "how much":

más	*bastante*	*mucho*
menos	*muy*	*poco*
demasiado	*casi*	*tanto*

Some adverbs of quantity are known to add a suffix in order to intensify the word's meaning. Look what happens here to the spelling:

Poco	+	*-ito*	→	*Quiero un* <u>*poquito*</u>. (I want a very small amount.)
Mucho	+	*-ísimo*	→	*Te amo* <u>*muchísimo*</u>. (I love you very, very much.)

¿Quieres Practicar?

Create a sentence or phrase using each of the following adverbs:

1. *más* _____

2. *menos* _____

3. *muy* _____

4. *mucho* _____

5. *poco* _____

HOW TO GET AN A+

Review this summary of the important parts of speech we studied in this chapter.

<u>Demonstrative Adjectives</u>: "this, that, these, or those" (at three different locations)

<u>Demonstrative Pronouns</u>: "this or that one, these or those ones" (with accent marks)

<u>Possessive Adjectives: Short-Form</u>: *mi/mis, tu/tus, su/sus, nuestro/nuestros, su/sus*

<u>Possessive Pronouns</u>: Take place of noun (*el mío, la tuya,* etc.)

<u>Personal Pronouns</u>:

1. <u>Subject Pronouns</u>: The subject of a verb (*yo, tú,* etc.)
2. <u>Prepositional Pronouns</u>: The object of a preposition (*para mí, para ti,* etc.)
3. <u>Direct Object Pronouns</u>: Answer the questions "what?" or "whom?" with regard to what the subject of the sentence is doing (*me, te, lo, la, nos, los, las*)
4. <u>Indirect Object Pronouns</u>: Tell where the D.O. is going (*me, te, le, nos, les*)
5. <u>Double Object Pronouns</u>:
   A. I.O. before D.O. and they can't be split
   B. No two *L* words in a row
   C. Clarify *se* with *A* + PREPOSITIONAL PRONOUN!

<u>Relative Pronouns</u>: (*que, quien, el que, el cual,* and after prepositions)

1. Take two related sentences
2. Replace the noun in the second sentence with the relative pronoun
3. Insert the new relative clause (which begins with the relative pronoun)

<u>Prepositions</u>: (*a, de, con, en, por, para,* etc.)

1. Using the preposition *de*: description, possession, origin, composition, content, movement, or cause
2. Using the preposition *a*: motion, personal
3. Using the preposition *con*: accompaniment, possession, description, method, or relationship
4. Using the preposition *en*: location and time, part of verb infinitives
5. Using the prepositions *Por* and *Para*: POR Back ; PARA Forward

<u>Adverbs</u>: Modify verbs, adjectives, other adverbs (many end with *-mente*)

1. Adverbs of manner: *rápidamente*
2. Adverbs of time: *mañana*
3. Adverbs of place: *aquí*
4. Adverbs of quantity: *mucho*

> You may not feel very confident yet, so look back at the
> last few chapters and see how your skills have grown!

Chapter 6
Capítulo Seis

Verbs
Los Verbos

INTRODUCTION TO VERBS

Your grade will soar once you understand verbs in Spanish. Here are the fundamentals:

- The basic form of a Spanish verb is called an infinitive, which may have three obvious endings: *-ar* [e.g., *hablar* (to speak)], *-er* [e.g., *correr* (to run)], and *-ir* [e.g., *vivir* (to live)]. However, verbs are generally used in conjugated forms of the infinitive in order to express a specific tense or time (present, future, past).

- There are three major classes of verbs in Spanish and they are all used differently:

  1. <u>Transitive (or Active) verbs</u>, which require a direct object—e.g., *pegar* (to hit)
  2. <u>Intransitive verbs</u>, which normally don't have a direct object—e.g., *correr* (to run)
  3. <u>Linking verbs</u>, which often connect subjects to everything else—e.g., *ser* (to be)

- There are three "persons" in Spanish: if either "I" or "We" participate in an action, it is called the "first person." If an informal "you" or "you guys" participate in an action, it is called the "second person." And lastly, if the formal "you," "you all," "he," "she," "it," or "they" participate in an action, it is called the "third person." Remember too that a person can be either singular or plural. This is called "number" in Spanish.

- Verbs also have two other grammatical properties that are important: their "mood" (indicative, imperative, subjunctive) and their "voice" (active, passive). These will be discussed in more detail later, so for the time being, just remember that most of the time people speak in the indicative mood and active voice.

- Some Spanish verbs are called "reflexive," where the infinitive ends in *se* and include reflexive pronouns in their conjugations, for example, *lavarse* (to wash oneself). They are called reflexive because the subject and the object are the same; that is, the verb "reflects" upon itself. Sentences using reflexive verbs are a lot like English reflexives, but the order of words is generally reversed. That's why students struggle with them. We'll look at the use of *se* words in more detail in Chapter 7: Tough Topics.

¡OYE!

Some textbooks list two other kinds of verbs out there, so we'll be sure to cover them:

Impersonal verbs: *No <u>hay</u> tiempo.*
                There's no time.

Helping or auxiliary verbs: *Está mal <u>haber</u> comido eso.*
                         It's not good that you've eaten that.

¿*Quieres Practicar?*

1. What are the three moods in Spanish?

2. Give an example of person and number.

3. Name the three primary endings of verb infinitives in Spanish.

4. How many different voices are there?

5. What is a reflexive verb in Spanish?

¡CONVERSEMOS!

Here are some tips about learning Spanish verbs:

1. Learn -*ar* verbs because they make up 80% of the language.
2. Learn irregular verbs cautiously, because they create most of the problems for students.
3. Learn some of the hundreds of verbs that look like English.
4. Learn those verbs that you can experiment with in everyday real-life activities.
5. Learn lots of verbs that are considered regular and easy to conjugate.

THE SIMPLE PRESENT TENSE

The simple present tense in Spanish generally describes an action that takes place now or on a regular basis, but can refer to a future time if it is mentioned in the sentence:

Juan Carlos trabaja mucho (hoy).
- Juan Carlos works a lot.
- Juan Carlos will work a lot (today).
- Juan Carlos is working a lot.

To form the negative in the present tense, as with all tenses, insert "*no*" in front of the verb: *Juan Carlos no come mucho.* (Juan Carlos doesn't eat much.) To form a question, either the subject is placed after the verb, or there is a change in intonation to a statement:

¿Come mucho Juan Carlos?

¿Juan Carlos come mucho?

Does Juan Carlos eat a lot?

¡OYE!

An inverted question mark always precedes any interrogation (question) in Spanish, and the helping words "do" and "does" in a question are not translated!

I. Simple Present Tense

The infinitives of Spanish verbs may end in *-ar*, *-er*, or *-ir*. Look at the box below and see how three typical *regular* verbs are conjugated in the simple present (indicative) tense. Again, don't fret about the *vosotros* conjugation, unless you plan to travel to Spain.

Subject Pronoun	HABLAR (to speak)	COMER (to eat)	ESCRIBIR (to write)
(yo)	hablo	como	escribo
(tú)	hablas	comes	escribes
(él, ella, Ud.)	habla	come	escribe
(nosotros)	hablamos	comemos	escribimos
(vosotros)	habláis	coméis	escribís
(ellos, ellas, Uds.)	hablan	comen	escriben

Write these endings down somewhere: *-o*, *-as*, *-a*, *-amos*, *áis*, *-an/-o*, *-es*, *-e*, *-emos* *(-imos)*, *-éis*, *-en*.

Notice that for the *-er* and *-ir* verbs, the conjugations are the same in the present tense, except for the *nosotros* and *vosotros* forms. This tense, which is the most common in Spanish and English, is called indicative because it's used primarily to make statements or ask questions. Also notice the difference between informal (**inf.**) and formal (**form.**) speech in Spanish: *Tú hablas español.* (inf. sing.), *Ud. habla español* (form. sing.).

¿Quieres Practicar?

Follow these examples, say the forms aloud, and make up some sample sentences:

Hablar: Hablo, Hablamos, Hablas, Habláis, Habla, Hablan   <u>Yo hablo inglés.</u>

Comer: Como, Comemos, Comes, Coméis, Come, Comen   <u>Pedro come tacos.</u>

Vivir: Vivo, Vivimos, Vives, Vivís, Vive, Viven   <u>Ellos viven aquí.</u>

1. *Estudiar:* _____   _____

2. *Correr:* _____   _____

3. *Escribir:* _____   _____

¡PALABRAS EXTRAS!

Try to add time-related vocabulary to complete your sentences:

Estudio . . .	I study . . .
con frecuencia	frequently
de vez en cuando	once in a while
generalmente	usually
casi nunca	seldom
nunca	never
siempre	always
todos los días	every day
todo el tiempo	all the time

Find any list of regular Spanish verbs and create a simple flashcard system:

1. On a white index card, print the name of a Spanish verb in large letters.
2. On the back, at the top, in small letters, write its meaning in English.
3. Below the translation, print the six conjugated forms of the verb clearly.

You should know what the conjugated forms mean since they always refer to the same person or thing (see the previous chart). Make as many white cards as you like, but be careful with your spelling! To avoid confusion, use a different colored card for each verb tense. Here's an example of regular -*ar* verbs in the present tense:

estudiar	**to study** estudio estudiamos estudias estudiáis estudia estudian

Now, start "flashing" your cards until you know them by heart. Try some with a friend!

¿Quieres Practicar?

Supply the correct verb form in the present tense. Look up any words you don't know:

1. *Jaime (comer) mucho.*   <u>*Jaime come mucho.*</u>

2. *Nosotros (apagar) las luces.*   _____

3. *¿(fumar) usted?*   _____

4. *Ellos no (beber) café.* _____

5. *Yo (comprar) la comida hoy.* _____

6. *¿Dónde (vivir) tú?* _____

7. *El señor Lara (vender) carros.* _____

8. *Nosotros (recibir) mucho correo.* _____

9. *¿Cuándo (viajar) ustedes?* _____

10. *El gato (correr) en el jardín.* _____

2. *apagamos*	5. *compro*	3. *Fuma*
8. *recibimos*	6. *vives*	9. *viajan*
	7. *vende*	10. *corre*
		4. *beben*

¡LEE Y ESCRIBE!

You can compare nouns with *tan*, but when two verbs are compared as equals, *tan* simply changes to *tanto*:

¡Es <u>tan</u> grande <u>como</u> Federico!
He's as big as Federico!

Sra. Nario cultiva flores <u>tanto como</u> su vecina.
Mrs. Nario plants flowers as much as her neighbor.

II. Simple Present Tense: Irregular Verbs

Start grouping sets of irregular verbs now, for easy study and/or review. Star pupils of Spanish know the shortcuts to learning all these changes, so let's try out a few:

A. PRESENT TENSE IRREGULARS: FIRST PERSON SINGULAR ONLY
-go, -zco, sé, veo, doy

1. **-GO** This first group has an irregular change in the first person (*yo*), and ends in the letters ("*-go*"):

poner (to put)

PON<u>GO</u>	*ponemos*
pones	*ponéis*
pone	*ponen*

caer (to fall); ***caigo***   *hacer* (to do or make); ***hago***

salir (to leave); ***salgo***   *traer* (to bring); ***traigo***

2. **-ZCO** Most verbs ending in *-ecer* and *-ucir* have the *-zco* ending:

   conducir (to drive)

CONDU<u>ZCO</u>	*conducimos*
conduces	*conducís*
conduce	*conducen*

   conocer (to know personally); ***conozco***   *obedecer* (to obey); ***obedezco***

   ofrecer (to offer); ***ofrezco***   *producir* (to produce); ***produzco***

3. **SÉ, VEO, DOY** These only have bizarre changes in the first person:

saber (to know)		***ver*** (to see)		***dar*** (to give)	
SÉ	*sabemos*	**VEO**	*vemos*	**DOY**	*damos*
sabes	*sabéis*	*ves*	*veis*	*das*	*dais*
sabe	*saben*	*ve*	*ven*	*da*	*dan*

¡OYE!

By the way, all verbs with the embedded word *poner*, like *suponer* (to suppose) are conjugated the same as *poner*: *supongo, suponemos*, etc. The same rule holds true for verbs with the embedded word *traer*, like *distraer* (to distract): *distraigo, distraemos*, etc., and the word *conocer*, like *reconocer* (to recognize): *reconozco, reconocemos*, etc.

¡SECRETOS!

Although both verbs *saber* and *conocer* mean to know, *conocer* implies that one is acquainted with, or knows someone or something with familiarity. *Saber*, on the other hand, means to know something as a result of mental effort, study, or training:

Yo le conozco.	I know him.
Yo sé leer español.	I know how to read in Spanish.

¿*Quieres Practicar?*

Answer these questions using the <u>first person singular</u> form:

1. ¿*Quién hace la comida?*   *Yo hago la comida.*

2. ¿*Quién trae el pelota?*   *Yo* _____

3. ¿*Quién obedece la ley?*   *Yo* _____

4. ¿*Quién sale temprano?*   *Yo* _____

5. ¿*Quién sabe hablar español?*   *Yo* _____

2. *traigo*   3. *obedezco*
4. *salgo*   5. *sé*

B. PRESENT TENSE IRREGULARS: PRIMARY STEM CHANGING

$$e \rightarrow ie, o \rightarrow ue, e \rightarrow i$$

These three stem-changers confuse learners, so pay attention. Look at the spelling change:

1. **E → IE**
   The middle *e* shifts to *ie* in all but the *nosotros* and *vosotros* forms:

entender (to understand)		*querer* (to want)	
entiendo	**entendemos**	quiero	**queremos**
entiendes	**entendéis**	quieres	**queréis**
entiende	entienden	quiere	quieren

2. **O → UE**
   The middle *o* shifts to *ue* in all but the *nosotros* and *vosotros* forms:

recordar (to remember)		*poder* (can, to be able to)	
recuerdo	**recordamos**	puedo	**podemos**
recuerdas	**recordáis**	puedes	**podéis**
recuerda	recuerdan	puede	pueden

3. **E → I**
   The middle *e* shifts to *i* in all but the *nosotros* and *vosotros* forms:

servir (to serve)		*repetir* (to repeat)	
sirvo	**servimos**	repito	**repetimos**
sirves	**servís**	repites	**repetís**
sirve	sirven	repite	repiten

¿Quieres Practicar?

Let's do a practice drill. Follow the example:

1. ¿Entiendes?   Sí, entiendo.
2. ¿Recuerdas?   _____
3. ¿Sirves?   _____
4. ¿Quieres?   _____
5. ¿Puedes?   _____

2. recuerdo   3. sirvo
4. quiero   5. puedo

C. PRESENT TENSE IRREGULARS:
REALLY RADICAL STEM CHANGING

The best option is to simply write these down somewhere. And watch out for the accent marks:

jugar (to play)

juego	jugamos
juegas	jugáis
juega	juegan

oler (to smell)

huelo	olemos
hueles	oléis
huele	huelen

reír (to laugh)

río	reímos
ríes	reís
ríe	ríen

sonreír (to smile)

sonrío	sonreímos
sonríes	sonreís
sonríe	sonríen

¡PALABRAS EXTRAS!

These two stem-changing verbs have only one form in the present tense due to their unique meanings:

llover (to rain)   *nevar* (to snow)
Llueve. It rains.   *Nieva.* It snows.

¿Quieres Practicar?

Follow the example.

1. It smells.   *Huele.*

2. It rains.   _____

3. It smiles.   _____

4. It plays.   _____

5. It laughs.   _____

2. *Llueve.*   3. *Sonríe.*
4. *Juega.*   5. *Ríe.*

D. PRESENT TENSE IRREGULARS:
WORDS ENDING IN *-uir, -iar, -uar*

This group always creates trouble for students because of the way the words are written and pronounced. Notice the unique letters in each one:

THE *y* WORDS
incluir (to include)

incluyo	**incluímos**
incluyes	**incluís**
incluye	incluyen

construir (to build)

construyo	**construímos**
construyes	**construís**
construye	construyen

THE *i* WORDS
enviar (to send)

envío	**enviamos**
envías	**enviáis**
envía	envían

THE *ú* WORDS
continuar (to continue)

continúo	**continuamos**
continúas	**continuáis**
continúa	continúan

¿Quieres Practicar?

If the verb form is correct, put *CORRECTO* and *INCORRECTO* if it is not:

1. It includes = *incluye*   *CORRECTO*

2. We send = *enviamos*   _____

3. They put = *pongen*   _____

4. He builds = *construyen*   _____

5. You continue = *continúas*   _____

3. I   1. C
4. I   2. C   5. C

E. PRESENT TENSE IRREGULARS: COMPLETELY RADICAL CHANGES

Some changes to verbs in the present tense make no sense at all, as we saw with *ser*, *estar*, and *tener*. The good news is that there are only a few others to remember:

ir (to go) ← similar to **dar**

voy	vamos
vas	vais
va	van

venir (to come) ← similar to **tener**

vengo	venimos
vienes	venís
viene	vienen

decir (to say, tell)

digo	decimos
dices	decís
dice	dicen

oír (to hear)

oigo	oímos
oyes	oís
oye	oyen

¿Quieres Practicar?

a.) Follow the example, insert a name, and then practice the present tense:

1. **Jaime** / *ir* / *a Chicago.*   *Jaime va a Chicago.*

2. _____ / *decir* / *muchos chistes.* _____

3. _____ / *venir* / *conmigo al supermercado.* _____

4. _____ / *tener* / *un perro grande.* _____

5. _____/ *no oír* / *la música.* _____

b.) Fill in one example from each of the five categories of irregular verbs in the present tense:

1. Three groups change in the first person singular or *yo* form: _____

2. Three groups have primary stem changes: _____

3. A couple of verbs have more radical changes in the stem: _____

4. Some verbs have the letters *y*, *i*, and *ú* inserted: _____

5. A few are totally radical and should be studied first: _____

F. VERBS WITH SPELLING CHANGES: *-jo, -go, -zo*

The following changes make perfect sense, because they only deal with the spelling. The change in the first person singular is made in order to create the correct pronunciation. Take care when you write these down:

1. **The -*jo* Words:** For verbs ending in *-ger* and *-gir*

recoger (to gather, pick up)		***dirigir*** (to direct)	
reco**jo**	recogemos	diri**jo**	dirigimos
recoges	recogéis	diriges	dirigís
recoge	recogen	dirige	dirigen

2. **The -*go* Words:** For verbs ending in *-guir*

distinguir (to distinguish)		***seguir*** (to follow)	
distin**go**	distinguimos	si**go**	seguimos
distingues	distinguís	sigues	seguís
distingue	distinguen	sigue	siguen

3. **The -*zo* Words:** Verbs ending in *-cer* or *-cir*

vencer (to conquer)		***torcer*** (to twist)	
ven**zo**	vencemos	tuer**zo**	torcemos
vences	vencéis	tuerces	torcéis
vence	vencen	tuerce	tuercen

¿Quieres Practicar?

Supply the correct present tense form of the verb:

1. *Yo (recoger) mi correo a las cinco.* _____recojo_____

2. *Nosotros (seguir) las instrucciones.* _____

3. *Yo (proteger) a mi familia.* _____

4. *El niño siempre (torcer) cosas.* _____

5. *¿Tú (dirigir) el tráfico?* _____

2. *seguimos*   3. *protejo*
4. *tuerce*   5. *diriges*

¡CONVERSEMOS!

By utilizing the following two constructions in conversation, the present tense can express actions that began in the past and continue into the present:

Hace _____ que _____.
Hace años que estudio inglés.   I've been studying English for years.
Hace semanas que no veo a Tomás.   I haven't seen Tomás for weeks.

_____ desde hace _____.
No fumo desde hace un mes.   I haven't smoked for a month.
Trabajo aquí desde hace dos días.   I've been working here for two days.

THE PAST TENSE: THE PRETERIT

Spanish has two basic past tenses—the **preterit** (*el pretérito*) and the **imperfect** (*el imperfecto*)—and you will need to know the difference in usage. The preterit is a bit more common, because it generally refers to actions that were completed in past time. It's also harder for students to learn:

I. The Preterit: Regular Verbs

-é,-aste,-ó,-amos,-asteis, -aron/-í,-iste,-ió,-imos, -isteis, -ieron

To form the preterit, these endings are added to the stem of regular verbs:

Subject Pronoun	HABLAR (to speak)	COMER (to eat)	ESCRIBIR (to write)
(yo)	hablé	comí	escribí
(tú)	hablaste	comiste	escribiste
(él, ella, Ud.)	habló	comío	escribío
(nosotros)	hablamos	comimos	escribimos
(vosotros)	hablasteis	comisteis	escribisteis
(ellos, ellas, Uds.)	hablaron	comieron	escribieron

Take note of both word ending patterns: *-é,-aste,-ó,-amos, -asteis, -aron/-í, -iste, -ió, -imos, isteis, -ieron*. The endings for *er* (*comer*) and *ir* (*escribir*) verbs are exactly the same. There are also lots of accent marks and you need to say them correctly. Check out the difference: *Yo hablo.* (I speak.), *Ella habló.* (She spoke.) Students get those two forms mixed up all the time.

To use the preterit, simply refer to what happened and was COMPLETED in the past:

Hablé con Francisco.	I spoke with Francisco.
Comimos a las doce.	We ate at twelve o'clock.
No escribieron mucho.	They didn't write much.

II. The Preterit: Irregular Verbs

A. PRETERIT IRREGULARS: 3rd PERSON

The present tense stem-changing verbs don't make those changes in the preterit, but look what happens with these in the 3rd person singular and plural:

repetir (to repeat)		**dormir** (to sleep)	
repetí	*repetimos*	*dormí*	*dormimos*
repetiste	*repetisteis*	*dormiste*	*dormisteis*
repitió	**repitieron**	**durmió**	**durmieron**

 ¿Quieres Practicar?

Change these sentences from the present to the preterit tense:

1. *Carlos toma café.*   *Carlos tomó café.*
2. *Vendemos el carro.*   _____
3. *¿Qué estudias?*   _____
4. *No viven aquí.*   _____
5. *Entiendo el ejercicio.*   _____
6. *El bebé duerme mucho.*   _____

2. *Vendimos*
3. *estudiaste*
4. *vivieron*
5. *Entendí*
6. *durmió*

B. PRETERIT IRREGULARS: DIRTY DOZEN

Although these "dirty dozen" have irregular stems that must be memorized, when you break them into groups of three most take similar endings in the preterit. Read each conjugation aloud:

tener	*estar*	*andar*	*querer*	*poner*	*hacer*
(to have)	(to be)	(to go, walk)	(to want)	(to put)	(to do, make)
tuve	estuve	anduve	quise	puse	hice
tuviste	estuviste	anduviste	quisiste	pusiste	hiciste
tuvo	estuvo	anduvo	quiso	puso	hizo**
tuvimos	estuvimos	anduvimos	quisimos	pusimos	hicimos
tuvisteis	estuvisteis	anduvisteis	quisisteis	pusisteis	hicisteis
tuvieron	estuvieron	anduvieron	quisieron	pusieron	hicieron

traer	*decir*	*traducir*	*saber*	*caber****	*venir*
(to bring)	(to say, tell)	(to translate)	(to know)	(to fit)	(to come)
traje	dije	traduje	supe	cupe	vine
trajiste	dijiste	tradujiste	supiste	cupiste	viniste
trajo	dijo	tradujo	supo	cupo	vino
trajimos	dijimos	tradujimos	supimos	cupimos	vinimos
trajisteis	dijisteis	tradujisteis	supisteis	cupisteis	vinisteis
trajeron*	dijeron*	tradujeron*	supieron	cupieron	vinieron

*Note that *traer*, *decir*, and *traducir* have stems ending in -*jeron* in the third person plural instead of the usual -*ieron*.
**Careful! The third person singular is *hizo* instead of *hico*.
***This verb is not used often, so you can memorize its forms later.

C. PRETERIT IRREGULARS: *ser, ver, dar, ir*

Beware A+ students! *Ser* (to be) and *ir* (to go) have identical preterit forms, but their meanings are understood when placed in context. The verb *dar* (to give) is similar to the regular verb *ver* (to see), and the secret here is to exclude all the accent marks:

	ser	*ir*	*dar*	*ver*
(yo)	fui	fui	di	vi
(tú)	fuiste	fuiste	diste	viste
(él, ella, Ud.)	fue	fue	dio	vio
(nosotros)	fuimos	fuimos	dimos	vimos
(vosotros)	fuisteis	fuisteis	disteis	visteis
(ellos, ellas, Uds.)	fueron	fueron	dieron	vieron

¿Quieres Practicar?

Translate into English:

1. *Yo fui a la fiesta.* _____

2. *No vi a Ricardo.* _____

3. *El programa fue terrible.* _____

4. *Le di el libro a Juana.* _____

5. *¿Adónde fue el taxi?* _____

3. The program was terrible.
2. I didn't see Ricardo.
1. I went to the party.
5. Where did the taxi go?
4. I gave the book to Juana.

¡OYE!

In some cases, the preterit tense may actually alter the meaning of a verb. Here are a few, but your textbook should list others you may need to know:

conocer (to know personally)	*Le conocí.*	I met him.
querer (to want)	*No quise ir.*	I refused to go.
saber (to know something)	*Supe la fecha.*	I found out the date.

D. VERBS WITH SPELLING CHANGES: *-car, -gar, -zar*

As we learned in the present tense, spelling changes in verb forms make perfect sense, because some sounds in Spanish can only be created by certain letters. These are only examples:

1. **-CAR**   ***explicar*** (to explain)

expli**qué**	explicamos
explicaste	explicasteis
explicó	explicaron

2. **-GAR**   ***llegar*** (to arrive)

lle**gué**	llegamos
llegaste	llegasteis
llegó	llegaron

3. **-ZAR**   ***cazar*** (to hunt)

ca**cé**	cazamos
cazaste	cazasteis
cazó	cazaron

E. VERBS WITH SPELLING CHANGES: *-yó/-yeron*

When the stem of an *-er* or *-ir* verb ends in *a, e, i, o,* or *-uir* (except *guir*), the following changes are made in the third person:

creer (to believe)

creí	*creímos*
creíste	*creísteis*
creyó	**creyeron**

oír (to hear)

oí	*oímos*
oíste	*oísteis*
oyó	**oyeron**

leer (to read)

leí	*leímos*
leíste	*leísteis*
leyó	**leyeron**

caer (to fall)

caí	*caímos*
caíste	*caísteis*
cayó	**cayeron**

incluir (to include)

incluí	*incluimos*
incluiste	*incluisteis*
incluyó	**incluyeron**

construir (to fall)

construí	*construimos*
construiste	*construisteis*
construyó	**construyeron**

¡LEE Y ESCRIBE!

Almost every Spanish student forgets these three spelling tips, so you might want to jot them down somewhere:

1. Verbs like *reír* (to laugh), *freír* (to fry), and *sonreír* (to smile) have a written accent mark on most of the forms in the preterit (e.g., *reí, reíste, rió, reímos, reísteis, rieron*).
2. *-ir* verbs with stems ending in *ñ* drop the i in the third person in the preterit [e.g., *gruñir* (to grunt)—*gruñó, gruñeron*].
3. Verbs ending in *-guar*, like *averiguar* (to investigate) change spelling in the first person singular in the preterit (*averigüé, averiguaste, averiguó, averiguamos, averiguasteis, averiguaron*).

¿Quieres Practicar?

a.) Write the first person singular form for each of these verbs:

1. *secar* (to dry)   (c)   ___sequé___

2. *alcanzar* (to reach)   (z)   _____

3. *colocar* (to place)   (c)   _____

4. *pegar* (to hit)   (g)   _____

5. *cruzar* (to cross)   (z)   _____

b.) Write the third person singular form for each of these verbs:

1. *leer* (to read)   *leyó*

2. *destruir* (to destroy)   _____

3. *proveer* (to provide)   _____

4. *obstruir* (to block)   _____

5. *poseer* (to possess)   _____

2. alcancé
3. coloqué
4. pegué
5. crucé

2. destruyó
3. proveyó
4. obstruyó
5. poseyó

THE PAST TENSE: THE IMPERFECT

The imperfect differs in usage and form from the preterit. Spanish students constantly struggle with knowing the difference, since they both refer to past time. Unlike the preterit, which expresses completed action in past time, the imperfect tense generally expresses repeated or continuous action. Instead of telling what you did, it tells what you were doing or used to do.

I. The Imperfect: Regular Verbs

-*aba* and -*ía*

These are the endings that are added to the stem of most verbs:

Subject Pronoun	**HABLAR** (to speak)	**COMER** (to eat)	**ESCRIBIR** (to write)
(yo)	*hablaba*	*comía*	*escribía*
(tú)	*hablabas*	*comías*	*escribías*
(él, ella, Ud.)	*hablaba*	*comía*	*escribía*
(nosotros)	*hablábamos*	*comíamos*	*escribíamos*
(vosotros)	*hablabais*	*comíais*	*escribíais*
(ellos, ellas, Uds.)	*hablaban*	*comían*	*escribían*

Look at the word-ending patterns: *-aba, -abas, -aba, -ábamos, -abais, -aban/-ía, -ías, -ía, -íamos, -íais, -ían*. The endings for the 1st person and 3rd person singular are the same, so you may need to specify. Instead of the preterit, which expresses COMPLETED action, tell what was happening or was REPEATED in the past:

Yo hablaba con Francisco.   I was speaking with Francisco.

Comíamos a las doce.   We used to eat at twelve o'clock.

No escribían mucho.   They wouldn't write much.

¿Quieres Practicar?

Write any form you like in the imperfect tense and then translate:

1. *votar* _____votábamos_____ ___we used to vote, we were voting___
2. *controlar* _____ _____
3. *absorber* _____ _____
4. *existir* _____ _____
5. *practicar* _____ _____

II. The Imperfect: Irregular Verbs

ir, ser, ver

Students like the imperfect because there are only three irregulars:

ir (to go)		**ser** (to be)		**ver** (to see)	
iba	íbamos	era	éramos	veía	veíamos
ibas	ibais	eras	erais	veías	veíais
iba	iban	era	eran	veía	veían

Here's how to use these three words in a typical sentence:

Yo iba a la iglesia con mi tía.	I used to go to church with my aunt.
Eran soldados muy valientes.	They were very brave soldiers.
Veíamos DVDs cuando él llegó.	We were watching DVDs when he arrived.

 ## ¿Quieres Practicar?

Insert the correct form of the imperfect on each line below:

1. (*comer*)   *Samuel _____ en el hotel con frecuencia.*
2. (*ir*)   *A veces los estudiantes _____ al parque.*
3. (*jugar*)   *Yo _____ con el perro todos los días.*
4. (*vivir*)   *Nosotros _____ cerca de un lago en las montañas.*
5. (*cantar*)   *¿ _____ mucho cuando era más joven?*
6. (*ir*)   *Yo _____ con ella a las fiestas.*
7. (*ver*)   *Tú siempre _____ televisión con la familia.*
8. (*bailar*)   *Martina _____ muy bien.*
9. (*hablar*)   *Cuando llegamos ellos _____ inglés.*
10. (*ser*)   *De vez en cuando yo _____ una persona muy seria.*

1. comía   2. iban   3. jugaba   4. vivíamos   5. cantaba   6. iba   7. veías   8. bailaba   9. hablaban   10. era

¡PALABRAS EXTRAS!

The preterit form of *hay* (there is, there are) is *hubo*, e.g., *Hubo un accidente*. (There was an accident.), and the imperfect form is *había* or *habían*, e.g., *Había una chica*. (There was one girl.), *Habían dos chicas*. (There were two girls.)

Here are a few more shortcuts to choosing the correct past tense:

1. Time phrases such as *con frecuencia*, *de vez en cuando*, and *muchas veces* often accompany the imperfect since they imply an unspecified period of time, whereas more concise terminology such as *ayer*, *anoche*, and *el otro día* often accompany the preterit.
2. Moods, emotions, and thoughts are also expressed with the imperfect tense, i.e., *¿Qué pensaba ella de mí?* (What did she think of me?).
3. The imperfect, and not the preterit, is used to tell what time it *was* in the past: *Eran las tres.* (It was three o'clock.).

¿Quieres Practicar?

Complete the translations using either the preterit or the imperfect:

1. They ate the pie. *(comer)* Ellos <u>comieron</u> /<u>comían</u> el pastel.

2. She washed dishes. *(lavar)* Ella _____ los platos.

3. We cleaned the bathroom. *(limpiar)* Nosotros _____ el baño.

4. I read several articles. *(leer)* Yo _____ muchos artículos.

5. You guys didn't go. *(ir)* Ustedes no _____ .

6. Who lived here? *(vivir)* ¿Quién _____ aquí?

7. It was a great party. *(ser)* _____ una fiesta muy buena.

8. Did you drink milk? *(beber)* ¿Tú _____ la leche?

THE FUTURE TENSE

The future tense refers to actions that take place in future time, though it may also be used in Spanish to express conjecture, probability, or inference in present time. For example, *¿Quién ganará?* could mean either "Who will win?" or "I wonder who might win?"

I. The Future Tense: Regular Verbs

-é, -ás, -á, -emos, -éis, -án

Most students learn this one quickly because you just add endings to the infinitive (not the stem) of regular verbs:

Subject Pronoun	HABLAR (to speak)	COMER (to eat)	ESCRIBIR (to write)
(yo)	hablaré	comeré	escribiré
(tú)	hablarás	comerás	escribirás
(él, ella, Ud.)	hablará	comerá	escribirá
(nosotros)	hablaremos	comeremos	escribiremos
(vosotros)	hablaréis	comeréis	escribiréis
(ellos, ellas, Uds.)	hablarán	comerán	escribirán

¡CONVERSEMOS!

Don't be concerned with some translations! It's not uncommon for the future tense to be replaced by the simple present tense when there is mention of some future time in the sentence. For example, both of these mean "He's coming Saturday":

Viene el sábado.   *Vendrá el sábado.*

¿Quieres Practicar?

Put the correct future tense form for each verb. You may need to look up a few meanings:

1. *manejar*   *(ellos)*   manejarán
2. *correr*   *(yo)*   _____
3. *caminar*   *(nosotros)*   _____
4. *ir*   *(ella)*   _____
5. *saltar*   *(tú)*   _____

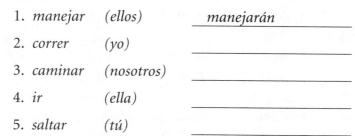

5. *saltarás*
4. *irá*
3. *caminaremos*
2. *correré*

II. The Future Tense: Irregular Verbs

saber, poner, decir

Break these irregularities into three main groups for easy study, though they aren't very common in everyday speech. Try to translate each word as you read aloud.

A. *sabré, podré, querré*

saber (to know)

sabré	sabremos
sabrás	sabréis
sabrá	sabrán

poder (to be able to)

podré	podremos
podrás	podréis
podrá	podrán

querer (to want)

querré	querremos
querrás	querréis
querrá	querrán

B. *pondré, saldré, tendré, vendré*

poner (to put)

pondré	pondremos
pondrás	pondréis
pondrá	pondrán

salir (to leave)

saldré	saldremos
saldrás	saldréis
saldrá	saldrán

tener (to have)

tendré	tendremos
tendrás	tendréis
tendrá	tendrán

venir (to come)

vendré	vendremos
vendrás	vendréis
vendrá	vendrán

C. *diré, haré*

decir (to say, tell)

diré	diremos
dirás	diréis
dirá	dirán

hacer (to do, make)

haré	haremos
harás	haréis
hará	harán

The most popular way to talk about the future in Spanish is with the construction *IR + A +* INFINITIVE: *Van a tener una fiesta.* (They're going to have a party.)

¿Quieres Practicar?

Change the underlined word from the past tense to the future tense:

1. *Ella <u>tenía</u> un apartamento en el centro.*   tendrá

2. *Ellos <u>hicieron</u> todo el trabajo.* _____

3. *Yo no <u>escribí</u> el e-mail.* _____

4. *¿Cuándo <u>veniste</u>?* _____

5. *Lo <u>puse</u> en el cuarto.* _____

2. *harán*   3. *escribiré*
4. *vendrás*   5. *pondré*

THE CONDITIONAL TENSE

The conditional tense is generally used to tell what would happen and refers to acts that are considered hypothetical in nature. In general, it either looks ahead to future time from the perspective of the past, or it expresses probability. As a rule, the conditional tense is used similarly in both Spanish and English. Take note, because you'll have to learn these three uses if you want to get an A+ in Spanish:

1. PAST → FUTURE: If the main verb of a sentence is in the past tense, the second verb is put into the conditional form when it denotes future action in the past: *Me <u>prometió</u> que <u>traería</u> el postre.* (He <u>promised</u> me that <u>he would bring</u> the dessert.)

2. PROBABILITY: The conditional tense is also used in Spanish to express conjecture, probability, or inference in past time: *¿Dónde estaría David?* (I wonder where David was?); *Sería las dos y media.* (It was probably two-thirty.)

3. COURTESY: The conditional form is often used to form more courteous expressions: *¿Podrías ayudarme?* (Could you help me?); *¿Saldríamos a comer?* (May we go out to eat?)

> **¡OYE!**
>
> STAY TUNED! The conditional tense is also used with the SUBJUNCTIVE mood, which will be explained in the next chapter. Notice the example:
>
> *Si yo fuera usted, no le hablaría.*
> I wouldn't talk to him if I were you.

I. The Conditional Tense: Regular Verbs

-ía, -ías, -ía, -íamos, -íais, -ían

Like the future tense, the endings that form the conditional in Spanish are the same for nearly all *-ar*, *-er*, and *-ir* verbs. These are added to the infinitive:

Subject Pronoun	HABLAR (to speak)	COMER (to eat)	ESCRIBIR (to write)
(yo)	hablaría	comería	escribiría
(tú)	hablarías	comerías	escribirías
(él, ella, Ud.)	hablaría	comería	escribiría
(nosotros)	hablaríamos	comeríamos	escribiríamos
(vosotros)	hablaríais	comeríais	escribiríais
(ellos, ellas, Uds.)	hablarían	comerían	escribirían

¿Quieres Practicar?

Change these present tense forms to the conditional:

1. *hablo*   <u>hablaría</u>   4. *vamos*   _____

2. *entiendes* _____   5. *comen*   _____

3. *juega* _____

2. entenderías   3. jugaría
4. iríamos   5. comerían

II. The Conditional Tense: Irregular Verbs

Like the future tense, the following verb infinitive forms are altered before the conditional tense endings are added. The root forms have the exact same changes, so you do it:

saber	**poder**	**querer**	**poner**	**salir**
sabr-	podr-	querr-	pond-	saldr-

tener	**venir**	**decir**	**hacer**	
tendr-	vendr-	dir-	har-	

Did you translate each verb form?

¡PALABRAS EXTRAS!

There are several other irregular verbs that fit into these groups. For example, verbs like *mantener* (to maintain) are like *tener*, *atraer* (to attract) like *traer*, and *deshacer* (to dissolve) like *hacer*. Here are two more examples:

valer (to be worth)

valdría	valdríamos
valdrías	valdríais
valdría	valdrían

suponer (to suppose)

supondría	supondríamos
supondrías	supondríais
supondría	supondrían

¿Quieres Practicar?

Translate into English:

1. *tú pondrías* — you would put

2. *ella podría* — _____

3. *ellos vendrían* — _____

4. *nosotros tendríamos* — _____

5. *yo haría* — _____

5. I would do or make
4. we would have
3. they would come
2. she would be able to

¡OYE!

The future and conditional tenses of *hay* (there is/are) are *habrá* (there will be) and *habría* (there would be), respectively. Generally, however, *HABER* is used as an auxiliary verb:

Habrá dos pájaros en la jaula.
There will be two birds in the cage.

Pensé que habría mucha gente en el estadio.
I thought there would be a lot of people in the stadium.

En cinco años, habrán ganado un partido.
In five years, they'll have won a game.

One way to improve your Spanish verb skills is to line up different tense forms in order to compare them. Soon you'll have the ability to recognize words that you read or hear. Fill in the missing forms of the verb tenses below:

PRESENT	PRETERIT	IMPERFECT	FUTURE	CONDITIONAL
tengo	*tuve*	*tenía*	*tendré*	*tendría*
pone	_____	_____	_____	_____
salen	_____	_____	_____	_____
decimos	_____	_____	_____	_____
haces	_____	_____	_____	_____
puedo	_____	_____	_____	_____
vienen	_____	_____	_____	_____
eres	_____	_____	_____	_____
vamos	_____	_____	_____	_____
sé	_____	_____	_____	_____

> Are you still checking off each section after you finish studying it? Many sections are divided into even smaller blocks of text to make the process easier.

THE PROGRESSIVE TENSES

estar + *-ndo*

This is a two-part verb, just as it is in English. The "progressive" tenses are used to describe actions or events that are currently in progress: *Estoy estudiando.* (I'm studying.) Here's how the two parts fit together.

I. The Progressive Tense, Part One: The Verb *estar*

First, use forms of the verb *estar* (to be) before verbs ending in *-ndo* (-ing). Forms of *estar* can reflect the present, past, future, or conditional tense:

Está	(He/she is)	
Estaba	(He/she was)	
Estuve	(He/she was)	} + *-ndo* (*-ando* or *-iendo*)
Estará	(He/she will be)	
Estaría	(He/she would be)	

II. The Progressive Tense, Part Two: The Present Participle

Second, add a verb ending in *-ando* or *-iendo*. Technically, they are called present participles, and are formed by adding *-ando* to the stem of *-ar* verbs and *-iendo* to the stems of *-er* and *-ir* verbs. They're easy once you practice with a few:

MAIN VERB	PRESENT PARTICIPLE	
hablar	*hab**lando***	(speaking)
comer	*com**iendo***	(eating)
escribir	*escrib**iendo***	(writing)
correr	_____	(running)
trabajar	_____	(working)
salir	_____	(leaving)

The key is choosing the correct form of *estar*: *Estoy trabajando, pero estaré descansando.* [I'm working (right now), but I'll be resting (later).] There are only a few irregular patterns you'll need to worry about forming in present participles: IR → *yendo*, SEGUIR → *siguiendo*, DORMIR → *durmiendo*. Students ALWAYS seem to forget about these!

¿Quieres Practicar?

a.) Change these infinitives to present participles and then say a sample sentence aloud:

1. *manejar* (to drive)   *manejando*_____

2. *escribir* (to write)   _____

3. *leer* (to read)   _____

4. *comenzar* (to start)   _____

5. *dormir* (to sleep)   _____

b.) Translate these sentences into Spanish using the progressive:

1. He was running.   *(correr)*   *Estaba corriendo.*_____

2. I am dancing.   *(bailar)*   _____

3. They will be arriving.   *(llegar)*   _____

4. She wouldn't be sleeping.   *(dormir)*   _____

5. Are you guys leaving?   *(salir)*   _____

2. *escribiendo*   4. *comenzando*   2. *Estoy bailando.*   5. *durmiendo*   4. *No estaría durmiendo.*   3. *Estarán llegando.*   5. *¿Están saliendo Uds.?*
3. *leyendo*   3. *escribiendo*

¡OYE!

Bear in mind that more complicated tenses of the verb *ESTAR* may also be used with a present participle, in order to express actions at various points in time:

Hemos estado usando la nueva computadora en la clase.
We have been using the new computer in the class.

Habría estado fumando, pero le quitamos sus cigarillos.
He would have been smoking, but we took away his cigarettes.

THE PERFECT TENSES

haber + -ado/-ido

Besides the progressives, there's another common two-part verb in Spanish. Just like English, the perfect tenses express a state or action as having been completed (perfected) at the time expressed by the helping verb *haber* (to have). The past participle of the main verb follows and completes the form, often ending in the letters *-ado* or *-ido*. Example: *He terminado.* (I have finished.) As a Spanish student, your biggest problem will be remembering the proper forms of *haber*.

I. The Present Perfect Tense, Part One

he, has, ha, hemos, habéis , han

Before anything else, the present tense forms of the irregular verb *haber* (to have) must be learned. They will express a current action that is still going on or repeated actions that have occurred in the past. Try reading these aloud:

	haber	(to have)
(yo)	*he*	I have
(tú)	*has*	you have (inf. sing.)
(él, ella, Ud.)	*ha*	you have (form. sing.), he, she, it has
(nosotros)	*hemos*	we have
(vosotros)	*habéis*	you have (inf. pl.)
(ellos, ellas, Uds.)	*han*	they, you (form. pl.) have

II. The Present Perfect Tense, Part Two: The Past Participle

A. THE PRESENT PERFECT TENSE: REGULAR VERBS

For most verbs, the past participle is formed as follows:

-AR verbs drop and change endings to *-ADO*:
llamar (to call) → *llamado* (called)

-ER and *-IR* verbs drop and change endings to *-IDO*:
aprender (to learn) → *aprendido* (learned)
permitir (to allow) → *permitido* (allowed)

B. THE PRESENT PERFECT TENSE: IRREGULAR VERBS *-to, -cho*

The following ten verbs have irregular past participles ending in *-to* and *-cho*. They are used a lot in Spanish, so create flash cards today.

COMMON VERBS WITH *-to* ENDINGS

escribir (to write)	*escrito* (written)
abrir (to open)	*abierto* (opened)
cubrir (to cover)	*cubierto* (covered)
poner (to put)	*puesto* (put)
volver (to return)	*vuelto* (returned)
romper (to break)	*roto* (broken)
morir (to die)	*muerto* (died)
ver (to see)	*visto* (seen)

VERBS WITH *-cho* ENDINGS

decir (to say, tell)	*dicho* (said, told)
hacer (to do, make)	*hecho* (done, made)

What's special about past participles is that although they form part of the perfect tenses—just as they do in English—their uses vary throughout the Spanish language: *El motor está <u>roto</u>.* (The engine is broken.), *No es <u>permitido</u>.* (It is not permitted.)

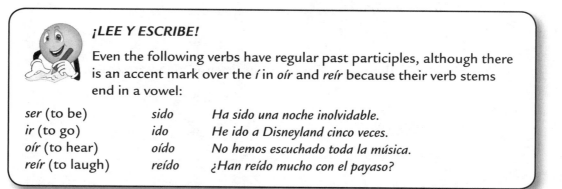

¡LEE Y ESCRIBE!

Even the following verbs have regular past participles, although there is an accent mark over the *í* in *oír* and *reír* because their verb stems end in a vowel:

ser (to be)	*sido*	*Ha sido una noche inolvidable.*
ir (to go)	*ido*	*He ido a Disneyland cinco veces.*
oír (to hear)	*oído*	*No hemos escuchado toda la música.*
reír (to laugh)	*reído*	*¿Han reído mucho con el payaso?*

¿Quieres Practicar?

Read each past participle and then fill in the correct infinitive:

1. *visto*	*ver*		6. *sido*		
2. *puesto*			7. *escrito*		
3. *ido*			8. *hecho*		
4. *tenido*			9. *estado*		
5. *vuelto*			10. *oído*		

2. *poner*   3. *ir*   4. *tener*
5. *volver*   6. *ser*   7. *escribir*
8. *hacer*   9. *estar*   10. *oír*

III. The Present Perfect Tense, Parts One and Two

Here's what it looks like when you put PARTS ONE and TWO together:

HABER
he
has
ha
hemos
habéis
han

HABLAR	***COMER***	***SALIR***	***DECIR***
hablado	*comido*	*salido*	*dicho*

¿Quieres Practicar?

a.) Add an appropriate word to complete these simple sentences:

1. *He hablado con _____.*   *He hablado con Juan.*

2. *¿Has comido la _____?*

3. *No han salido de _____.*

4. *Hemos estudiado _____ .*

5. *Lorenzo ha jugado _____.*

b.) Change these simple present tense verbs to the present perfect:

1. *vamos* (we go)   *hemos ido* (we have gone)

2. *trabajo* (I work)

3. *tiene* (he has)

4. *escriben* (they write) _____

5. *soy* (I am) _____

3. *ha tenido*   5. *he sido*

2. *he trabajado*   4. *han escrito*

III. The Past Perfect Tense

había, habías, había, habíamos, habíais, habían

If you truly want to sound like an A+ Spanish student, try using the past perfect (what many call the pluperfect or *el pluscuamperfecto*). Like the present perfect, it also requires TWO PARTS:

Ya <u>había lavado</u> el carro cuando comenzó a llover.
I already <u>had washed</u> the car when it began to rain.

The past perfect is used to express an action that happened in the past *before* another past action. Since it is used in relation to another past action, the other past action is ordinarily expressed in the preterit (in the example above, . . . *cuando <u>comenzó</u> a llover*). The pluperfect is formed by placing the imperfect tense of the verb *haber* before the past participle of the main verb:

(yo)	**había**			
(tú)	**habías**			
(él, ella, Ud.)	**había**	*TRABAJAR*	*CORRER*	*ESCRIBIR*
(nosotros)	**habíamos**	**trabajado**	**corrido**	**escrito**
(vosotros)	**habíais**			
(ellos, ellas, Uds.)	**habían**			

 ## ¿Quieres Practicar?

Change these present tense verb forms to the past perfect tense:

1. *comer (ella)*   <u>había comido</u>

2. *entender (yo)*   _____

3. *decir (ellas)*   _____

4. *ir (nosotros)*   _____

5. *hablar (Ud.)*   _____

6. *poner (yo)*   _____

7. *hacer (tú)*   _____

8. *ver (Uds.)*   _____

9. *venir (nosotros)*   _____

10. *estudiar (Él)*   _____

10. *había estudiado*   7. *habías hecho*   4. *habíamos ido*

9. *habíamos venido*   6. *había puesto*   3. *había dicho*

8. *habían visto*   5. *había hablado*   2. *había entendido*

By the way, to form a question in the perfect tenses, the subject pronoun follows the past participle, for example, *¿Dónde has trabajado tú?* (Where have you worked?). In the negative, the word *no* precedes the forms of the verb *haber*: *No habíamos jugado todavía.* (We hadn't played yet.) Also, whenever object pronouns are used with the present perfect, they precede the forms of the verb *haber*: *Ellos <u>me</u> <u>lo</u> han dicho.* (They have told me about it.)

¡OYE!

The past participle is used in the formation of all perfect tenses, where it remains the same regardless of person, number, or gender:

He <u>hecho</u> aquel trabajo muchas veces. (I have done that job many times.)
No habían <u>hecho</u> aquel trabajo antes. (They had not done that job before.)
¿Habrá <u>hecho</u> aquel trabajo? (Would he have the done the job?)

¡CONVERSEMOS!

Although seldom used in conversation, the preterit perfect tense in Spanish may replace the simple preterit. All the forms of HABER are in the preterit:

After they'd eaten, they went to work.
(Pret. Perf.) *Después de que <u>hubieron comido</u>, ellos fueron al trabajo.*
(Pret.) *Después de que <u>comieron</u>, ellos fueron al trabajo.*

IV. The Future Perfect and Conditional Perfect Tenses

To be honest, not many Spanish speakers use these tenses, but you'll still need to study them if you plan to get an A+ in Spanish. They can be easy as long as you know precisely when an action will take place.

A. THE FUTURE PERFECT TENSE

habrá

The future perfect is primarily used to describe an action that will take place before a specific time in the future or <u>before</u> some other future action, though it sometimes expresses probability in past time. Like all perfect tenses, the action will already be completed:

Sr. García <u>habrá firmado</u> el contrato para las tres.
Mr. García <u>will have signed</u> the contract by three o'clock.

Habrá tenido un accidente.
Maybe he had an accident.

As you can see, the future perfect is formed by placing the future tense of the irregular verb *haber* before the past participle of the main verb:

	+ Past Participle
habré	*habremos*
habrás	*habréis*
habrá	*habrán*

¿Quieres Practicar?

Change these verb forms in the future tense to the future perfect:

1. *tener (yo)*   _____habré tenido_____
2. *ir (tú)*   _____
3. *escribir (Ud.)*   _____
4. *decir (nosotros)* _____
5. *ver (ellos)*   _____

2. *habrás ido*   3. *habrá escrito*
4. *habremos dicho*   5. *habrán visto*

B. THE CONDITIONAL PERFECT TENSE

habría

The conditional perfect tense is more common, and describes events that would have been completed in the past. It also expresses probability or conjecture about a completed event from the past perspective:

Me dijeron que lo habrían hecho.
They told me that they would have done it.

Habrían bailado la salsa toda la noche.
They probably had danced the Salsa all night.

Learn these conditional forms of *haber* today:

	+ Past Participle
habría	*habríamos*
habrías	*habríais*
habría	*habrían*

¡OYE!

The conditional perfect is often used with hypothetical situations that would have taken place in the past if certain conditions—expressed in the IMPERFECT SUBJUNCTIVE—had been met. We'll learn more about this in the next chapter:

Si yo hubiera tenido un carro, habría pasado mis vacaciones en la playa.
If I would have had a car, I would have spent my vacation at the beach.

¿Quieres Practicar?

Try to read these sentences quickly in Spanish. If you like, do your best to translate them.

1. *Yo habría comido todo el helado.*
2. *Me contaron que habrían traído la familia, pero no había mucho tiempo.*
3. *Habrían sido las seis cuando ellos se fueron.*
4. *Sé que tú no lo habrías hecho solo.*
5. *Si hubiéramos tenido el dinero, lo habríamos comprado.*

¡PALABRAS EXTRAS!

You can use *HABER* all by itself with a past participle either as a complement to some verbs or after a preposition:

Mi hermano es mucho más fuerte por <u>haber tomado</u> sus vitaminas.
My brother is much stronger for having taken his vitamins.

This so-called perfect infinitive can be used in different ways. For example, the construction *DEBER DE* + perfect infinitive is used to express probability:

Sandra <u>debe de haber perdido</u> las llaves.
Sandra must have (probably) lost the keys.

HOW TO GET AN A+

The bottom line is students cannot be successful in Spanish without knowing verbs. However, understanding basic verb conjugations is not enough! You'll also need to know how to use them.

Spanish verbs are generally used in tenses, which means messages can shift to and from any past, current, or future activity. The tenses we've learned in this chapter can be grouped into four main categories:

1. **Present Tense**
2. **Past Tenses**
3. **Future and Conditional Tenses**
4. **Progressive and Perfect Tenses**

The only way to burn these into your memory is to continually practice them. That means you'll need to go through this chapter again, spending more time on those explanations that may have confused you. It also means you might have to go on-line to search for more examples and review. Your success will depend on how much you effectively experiment with verbs, correct your mistakes, and then try them out again. Remember that without learning verb tenses, you can't really communicate in Spanish.

Chapter 7
Capítulo Siete

Tough Topics
Temas Problemáticos

THE SUBJUNCTIVE

Let's open our study of the dreaded subjunctive with three important statements:

1. Every Spanish verb tense introduced in the previous chapters has allowed you to form sentences in something called the indicative "mood," which only means that **everything stated was based on fact and certainty**: *Carlos trabaja a las dos.* (Carlos works at two.)

2. The subjunctive mood, however, expresses **certain changes in the speaker's attitude or emotion**, which is why it is often referred to as the "unreal" mode. As a result, the verbs change in form, which we'll discuss in detail just ahead.

3. The basic forms of the subjunctive include both the present and the past tenses, but the real key to learning this mood is to know those other words that are usually associated with it. "WEDDING" is an acronym used for remembering when to switch over to the subjunctive:

W — Wish/Will: with verbs that express a desire, like *querer*: *Quiero que . . .* (I desire that . . .)

E — Emotion: with verbs that express emotion, like *temer*: *Temo que . . .* (I fear that . . .)

D — Doubt: with the verb *dudar*: *Dudo que . . .* (I doubt that . . .)

D — Denial: with the verb *negar*: *Niego que . . .* (I deny that . . .)

I — Impersonal: with impersonal expressions like *Es mejor que . . .* (It's better that . . .)

N — Negation: with verbs like *creer* (to believe) and *pensar* (to think) in negative sentences like *No creo que . . .* (I don't believe that . . .)

G — God: with *Ojalá que . . .* (I hope that . . .) or literally "May God grant that . . ."

I. The Present Subjunctive

The present subjunctive is used when the speaker wants to comment on either the present or future time. It is usually expressed in dependent noun clauses introduced by the conjunction *que* (that). These dependent clauses follow main clauses that express a variety of messages—from emotion and doubt to insistence and advice. Keep it simple by splitting your subjunctive sentences in two:

*Yo dudo / que **hablen** español bien.* [I doubt /(that) they can speak Spanish well.]
main clause   dependent clause

A. THE PRESENT SUBJUNCTIVE: REGULAR VERBS

ar → e; er, ir → a

To form the present subjunctive in regular verbs, simply change the vowel *a* of the present indicative to *e* in -*ar* verbs, and the vowels *e* and *i* to *a* in -*er* and –*ir* verbs:

Subject Pronoun	**HABLAR** (*to speak*)	**COMER** (*to eat*)	**ESCRIBIR** (*to write*)
(*yo*)	**hable**	**coma**	**escriba**
(*tú*)	**hables**	**comas**	**escribas**
(*él, ella, Ud.*)	**hable**	**coma**	**escriba**
(*nosotros*)	**hablemos**	**comamos**	**escribamos**
(*vosotros*)	**habléis**	**comáis**	**escribáis**
(*ellos, ellas, Uds.*)	**hablen**	**coman**	**escriban**

¡LEE Y ESCRIBE!

The present subjunctive forms include the same forms for the formal commands of Spanish:

<u>Hable</u> con Juan.	Talk to Juan.
<u>Coma</u> la comida.	Eat the food.
<u>Escriba</u> la palabra.	Write the word.

¿Quieres Practicar?

Change the present indicative to the present subjunctive:

1. *estudio →*   <u>estudie</u>

2. *come →*   _____

3. *escriben →*   _____

4. *vivo →*   _____

5. *bailamos →*   _____

2. *coma*   3. *escriban*   4. *viva*   5. *bailemos*

As the "wedding" acronym indicates, the present subjunctive is also used with impersonal expressions such as *es posible que, es importante que, es fantástico que,* etc. These too are also combined with a dependent noun clause to express a state or event that is **unreal, uncertain, or not actually true**:

Es posible que corran con mis amigos.	It's possible they might run with my friends.
Es importante que limpiemos la casa.	It's important we clean the house.

In most cases, the main clause of a subjunctive sentence signals that the mood has changed, and it takes special verbs to do so. These are just some of the many that are available:

1. TO EXPRESS COMMAND OR DESIRE: <u>*Quiero*</u> *que venga.* (I want you to come.) Examples: *querer* (to want), *preferir* (to prefer), *mandar* (to order), *exigir* (to demand), *desear* (to desire), *pedir* (to ask for), *sugerir* (to suggest), *esperar* (to hope), *suplicar* (to implore).

2. TO EXPRESS EMOTION OR ATTITUDE: <u>*Temo*</u> *que venga.* (I fear that he comes). Examples: *sorprender* (to surprise), *temer* (to fear), *gustar* (to like), *alegrarse* (to be happy), *tener miedo de* (to fear), *lamentar* (to be sad), *sentir* (to be sorry)

3. TO EXPRESS DOUBT, DENIAL, OR REFUSAL: <u>*Dudo*</u> *que venga.* (I doubt that he comes.) Examples: *dudar* (to doubt), *negar* (to deny), *prohibir* (to prohibit), *no pensar* (to not think), *no creer* (to not believe), *no imaginarse* (to not imagine), *no estar seguro* (to not be sure).

See how the verb of the main clause often causes another person or thing to act (or not act) in the dependent clause: *(**Yo**) prefiero/ que (**ella**) me escriba.* (I prefer that she writes me.)

¡CONVERSEMOS!

The verbs in the main clause of a sentence in the present subjunctive may be in the <u>present</u>, <u>present perfect</u>, or <u>future tense</u>, or in the <u>imperative</u> (command) mood:

Queremos que le digan.	We want you guys to tell her.
Han dudado que puedas cocinar.	They have doubted that you can cook.
Insistiré que no maneje.	I will insist that he does not drive.
Dígale que ponga la silla aquí.	Tell him to put the chair here.

¿Quieres Practicar?

Write the correct form of the present subjunctive on the line provided:

1. *(hablar)*   *Dudo que ella ____ español.* <u>*hable*</u>

2. *(comer)*   *Esperamos que ellos ____ la ensalada.*

3. *(escribir)*   *Es importante que tú ____ rápido.*

4. *(visitar)*   *No creemos que Sr. Mora ____ hoy.*

5. *(correr)*   *Ella quiere que nosotros____a la casa.*

B. THE PRESENT SUBJUNCTIVE: IRREGULAR VERBS

As you may recall, the simple present tense (indicative) is full of unusual verb conjugations. Well, most of those same stem-changing and irregular changes are similar in the simple present tense subjunctive. Just remember that most verbs with changes in the first person keep that form in the third person also:

cerrar	*Espero que él **cierre** las puertas.*	I hope he closes the doors.
volver	*Nos encanta que **vuelva** Ud. hoy.*	We're happy you return today.
pedir	*Prefiero que se lo **pida** a él.*	I prefer that you ask him for it.
conocer	*Quiere que lo **conozcas**.*	He wants you to know him.
construir	*Dudamos que lo **construyan**.*	We doubt that they'll build it.
ver	*Temo que me **vea** ella.*	I fear she'll see me.
caer	*Esperamos que no **caigan**.*	We hope they don't fall down.

This is a complete list of the most common irregular subjunctive forms in Spanish, so take notice! Look how all of them are derived from the 1st person, present indicative:

VERB INFINITIVE	1st PERSON PRES. INDIC.	ALL FORMS: PRES. SUBJ.
decir	*(digo)*	*diga, digas, diga, digamos, digáis, digan*
hacer	*(hago)*	*haga, hagas, haga, hagamos, hagáis, hagan*
oír	*(oigo)*	*oiga, oigas, oiga, oigamos, oigáis, oigan*
poner	*(pongo)*	*ponga, pongas, ponga, pongamos, pongáis, pongan*
salir	*(salgo)*	*salga, salgas, salga, salgamos, salgáis, salgan*
tener	*(tengo)*	*tenga, tengas, tenga, tengamos, tengáis, tengan*
traer	*(traigo)*	*traiga, traigas, traiga, traigamos, traigáis, traigan*
venir	*(vengo)*	*venga, vengas, venga, vengamos, vengáis, vengan*

¡LEE Y ESCRIBE!

Although *morir* and *dormir* have the *o → ue* stem change, there is a *u* in the first-person and second-person plural forms (e.g., *muera, mueras, muera, muramos, muráis, mueran*). Also, in the present subjunctive, most verbs that end in *-iar* or *-uar* have an accent mark on the *í* or *ú* in all forms but the first-person plural, so you'll need to really stress that syllable when you speak:

vaciar (to empty)	*vacíe, vacíes, vacíe, vaciemos, vaciéis, vacíen*
graduar (to graduate)	*gradúe, gradúes, gradúe, graduemos, graduéis, gradúen*

The following three verbs are quite unique and should be learned separately. Though their endings are regular, their stems are irregular in the present subjunctive:

VERB	STEM		EXAMPLE
ir	*vay…*	*vaya, vayas, vaya, vayamos, vayáis, vayan*	*Espero que Ud. vaya.*
saber	*sep…*	*sepa, sepas, sepa, sepamos, sepáis, sepan*	*Quiero que lo sepas.*
ser	*se…*	*sea, seas, sea, seamos, seáis, sean*	*Prefiero que sea ella.*

Memorize these patterns today! Other than the stem changes, irregular verb "endings" are generally the same in the present subjunctive:

-AR verbs	*-e, -es, -e, -emos, -éis, -en*
-ER, -IR verbs	*-a, -as, -a, -amos, -áis, -an*

¿Quieres Practicar?

Finish translating these sentences into English and then read both sentences aloud:

1. *Quiero que <u>conozcas</u> a mi familia.*   ＿＿＿ you to know my family.   <u>I want</u>

2. *Insistimos en que tú nos <u>veas</u>.*   We insist that ＿＿＿ us.   ＿＿＿＿＿

3. *<u>Espero</u> que construyan la pared.*   ＿＿＿ they build the wall.   ＿＿＿＿＿

4. *Le exigen que lo <u>haga ella</u>.*   They demand that ＿＿＿ it.   ＿＿＿＿＿

5. *Dudo que <u>él tenga</u> dos carros.*   I doubt ＿＿＿ two cars.   ＿＿＿＿＿

3. I hope	5. he has
2. you see	4. she does

C. THE PRESENT SUBJUNCTIVE: SPELLING CHANGES

There are a few spelling changes in the present subjunctive, but the forms sound normal when you say them:

-AR verbs

$G \rightarrow GU$	PEGAR (to hit, stick)	*Esperamos que pe**gu**e la pelota.*
$C \rightarrow QU$	PESCAR (to fish)	*Me alegro que pes**qu**en allí.*
$Z \rightarrow C$	EMPEZAR (to begin)	*Quiero que empe**c**emos a las dos.*

-ER, -IR verbs

$G \rightarrow J$	RECOGER (to pick up)	*Es importante que reco**j**amos la basura.*
$GU \rightarrow G$	SEGUIR (to follow)	*Dudo que si**g**a el camino.*
$C \rightarrow Z$	CONVENCER (to convince)	*Prefiere que ella lo conven**z**a.*

¡PALABRAS EXTRAS!

The verbs *DAR* and *ESTAR* are considered irregular only because of the accent marks. The first and third person singular of *DAR* have accents to differentiate them from the preposition *de*:

DAR dé, des, dé, demos, deis, den

ESTAR esté, estés, esté, estemos, estéis, estén

Espero que me <u>dé</u> el libro.   I hope he gives me the book.

Dudamos que <u>esté</u> en casa.   We doubt he is at home.

D. SHORTCUT TO THE SUBJUNCTIVE

First, memorize your formal commands:

¡Estudie!   Study!

¡Vengan!   Come, you guys!

¡Maneje!   Drive!

Second, practice those words in simple command phrases that begin with the word *Que*. Notice the translations:

¡<u>Que</u> estudie!   Go study!

¡<u>Que</u> vengan todos!   Everyone come!

¡<u>Que</u> maneje con cuidado!   Drive carefully!

Third, open with a phrase that expresses desire, doubt, emotion, or an impersonal thought:

<u>*Espero*</u> *que estudie.*   I hope you study.

<u>*Temo*</u> *que vengan todos.*   I'm afraid they'll all come.

<u>*Es importante*</u> *que maneje con cuidado.*   It's important that you drive carefully.

¿Quieres Practicar?

Use each impersonal expression to create a sentence in the subjunctive:

1. *Los gatos corren en el jardín. (Es malo)*

   Es malo que los gatos corran en el jardín.

2. *Los niños lloran mucho. (Es triste)*

3. *No trabajan en la oficina. (Es raro)*

_____

4. *Aprenden mucho español. (Es importante)*

_____

5. *Ellos vienen al mediodía. (Es probable)*

_____

5. *Es probable que vengan al mediodía.*
4. *Es importante que aprendan mucho español.*
3. *Es raro que no trabajen en la oficina.*
2. *Es triste que los niños lloren mucho.*

II. The Past Subjunctive

The past or what is called the imperfect subjunctive is used in the same way as the present subjunctive, but the basic difference is that the verb in the main clause is either in the past (imperfect, preterit, past perfect) or in the conditional tense. You may need to review these tenses from the previous chapter, because this form of the subjunctive is pretty common:

Imperfect: *Pedían que lo comprara.* (They were asking him to buy it.)

Preterit: *Pidieron que lo comprara.* (They asked him to buy it.)

Past Perfect: *Habían pedido que lo comprara.* (They had asked him to buy it.)

Conditional: *Pedirían que lo comprara.* (They would ask him to buy it.)

As was the case for the present subjunctive, notice how the subjects in the main and dependent clauses are different in the past subjunctive: *Ella* *quería /que* *tú* *trabajaras.* (She wanted you to work.)

🌹😊 **¡SECRETOS!**

The imperfect subjunctive forms of the verbs *QUERER*, *DEBER*, and *PODER* are often used to express requests or suggestions in a polite manner:

¿Quisieran ordenar más fruta?   Would they like to order more fruit?
Debiéramos ir al mercado.   It might be best if we go to the market.
¿Pudieras hacerme un favor?   Would you please do me a favor?

The base form of the past subjunctive is taken from the third person plural of the preterit, which includes all stem changes and irregularities. The *-ron* ending is dropped and the following endings are added:

TRABAJAR (to work)

3rd p. pl. of the preterit	=	**trabajaron**	**comieron**	**dijeron**
(yo)	**-ra**	*(trabajara)*	*(comiera)*	*(dijera)*
(tú)	**-ras**	*(trabajaras)*		
(él, ella, Ud.)	**-ra**	*(trabajara)*		
(nosotros)	**-ramos**	*(trabajáramos)*		
(vosotros)	**-rais**	*(trabajarais)*		
(ellos, ellas, Uds.)	**-ran**	*(trabajaran)*		

¡OYE!

A second imperfect subjunctive form exists in Spanish, but it is seldom used in everyday speech. These forms are interchangeable with the ones above:

TRABAJAR *(trabaja<u>ron</u>)*

(yo)	-se	*(trabajase)*
(tú)	-ses	*(trabajases)*
(él, ella, Ud.)	-se	*(trabajase)*
(nosotros)	-semos	*(trabajásemos)*
(vosotros)	-seis	*(trabajaseis)*
(ellos, ellas, Uds.)	-sen	*(trabajasen)*

¿Quieres Practicar?

Change these dependent noun clauses from the present subjunctive to the imperfect subjunctive:

3rd p. pl. pret.

1. *que yo estudie*	*(estudiaron)*	*que yo estudiara*
2. *que él quiera*		
3. *que ustedes den*		
4. *que nosotros salgamos*		
5. *que ellas tengan*		

2. (quisieron)   *que él quisiera*
3. (dieron)   *que ustedes dieran*
4. (salieron)   *que nosotros saliéramos*
5. (tuvieron)   *que ellas tuvieran*

III. The Present Perfect Subjunctive

haya- + Past Participle

Although it's not used as often, the present perfect indicates that the action in the dependent clause occurs before the action of the main clause: *Dudo que ellos hayan llegado.* (I doubt they have arrived.)

The present perfect subjunctive is formed by combining the present subjunctive of the verb *haber* with the past participle. All these forms include *haya-*, which implies might have:

HABER	*HABLAR*	*COMER*	*ESCRIBIR*
haya	*hablado*	*comido*	*escrito*
hayas			
haya			
hayamos			
hayáis			
hayan			

¿Quieres Practicar?

Change these from the present to the present perfect subjunctive, and then translate aloud:

1. *No creo que él <u>compre</u> gasolina.*   <u>*haya comprado*</u>

2. *Dudamos que <u>comas</u> mucho.*   _____

3. *Es posible que ellos <u>vengan</u>.*   _____

4. *Ella quiere que <u>esperemos</u> aquí.*   _____

5. *¿Piensas que ella <u>sea</u> honesta?*   _____

2. *hayas comido*   3. *hayan venido*
4. *hayamos esperado*   5. *haya sido*

IV. The Past Perfect Subjunctive

hubiera + Past Participle

This tense is used either to indicate an event that took place prior to something in the past or a hypothetical situation that could have happened, but didn't. This means that the main verb refers to the past and is usually expressed by the imperfect, preterit, or past perfect tense. Once you are familiar with those tenses, the rest of the sentence is a breeze:

Esperaban que hubiera hablado.	They were hoping that she had spoken.
Dudó que hubiéramos comido.	He doubted that we had eaten.
Había temido que hubieras salido.	I had feared that you had left.

The past perfect subjunctive is formed by combining the imperfect subjunctive of the verb *haber* with the past participle of the main verb. All these forms of *hubiera-* imply "might have had":

HABER	HABLAR	COMER	ESCRIBIR
hubiera	*hablado*	*comido*	*escrito*
hubieras			
hubiera			
hubiéramos			
hubierais			
hubieran			

¿Quieres Practicar?

Fill in the correct form of the verb *haber*:

1. *Esperaba que Ud. lo* __hubiera__ *tomado.*

2. *Me dijo que tú lo* _____ *tomado.*

3. *Era posible que ellos lo* _____ *tomado.*

4. *Yo dudaba que ella lo* _____ *tomado.*

5. *Temían que tú y yo lo* _____ *tomado.*

2. *hubieras*   3. *hubieran*   4. *hubiera*   5. *hubiéramos*

¡PALABRAS EXTRAS!

A future subjunctive tense exists in Spanish, but it is primarily found in literature. It carries the same meaning as the present subjunctive:

	HABLAR	COMER	ESCRIBIR
(yo)	hablare	comiere	escribiere
(tú)	hablares	comieres	escribieres
(él, ella, Ud.)	hablare	comiere	escribiere
(nosotros)	habláremos	comiéremos	escribiéremos
(vosotros)	hablarais	comiereis	escribiereis
(ellos, ellas, Uds.)	hablaren	comieren	escribieren

V. The Past Subjunctive: Conditional Sentences

si- Clauses

The past perfect subjunctive is also used in conditional sentences, which are found everywhere in Spanish. A conditional sentence consists of two clauses—a dependent clause beginning with *si* (if) and a main clause: *Si tienes una fiesta, llegaré temprano.* (If you have a party, I will arrive early.) Just remember that the word "if" lets you know that the sentence is conditional.

However, if there is some "unreal" or contrary-to-fact situation taking place in present time, the past perfect subjunctive is used in the *si*-clause, and the conditional tense is used in the main clause. Notice how the action is based entirely on something unknown or unsure: *Si trabajaras, te pagaría.* (If you would work, I would pay you.)

To express this same situation in past time, either the conditional perfect or past perfect subjunctive is used in the main clause, and the past perfect subjunctive is used in the *si*-clause: *Si hubieras trabajado, te habría* (or *hubiera*) *pagado.* (If you would have worked, I would have paid you.) The good news is that with conditional sentences, the order of the two clauses can be reversed and keep the same meaning: *Te habría pagado si hubieras trabajado.* What also helps is that these structures are similar in both languages:

Si yo hubiera estudiado, habría pasado el examen. (conditional perfect)
If I would have studied, I would have passed the exam.

Hubiéramos pintado la casa si hubieras comprado la pintura. (past perfect subjunctive)
We would have painted the house if you would have bought the paint.

 ## *¿Quieres Practicar?*

All of these open with the conditional perfect tense. Write the correct past perfect subjunctive forms on the lines provided:

1. *Habría ido a la playa si ella* __hubiera aprendido__ *nadar. (APRENDER)*

2. *Habrías llegado a tiempo si, _____ más rápido. (MANEJAR)*

3. *Habríamos celebrado si ellos _____ . (GANAR)*

4. *Nos habría llamado si nosotros _____ en casa. (ESTAR)*

5. *Habría plantado flores si él _____ tiempo. (TENER)*

2. *hubieras manejado*
3. *hubieran ganado*
4. *hubiéramos estado*
5. *hubiera tenido*

VI. Other Uses of the Subjunctive

A. ADVERBIAL CLAUSES

The subjunctive is also used in two other areas in Spanish—with adverbs and adjectives. The key here is to remember that any sentence with the subjunctive expresses uncertainty. Let's first look at some adverbial clauses. Conjunctions like *a fin de que* (in order that), *sin que* (without), *a menos que* (unless), *con tal de que* (provided that), *para que* (so that), *en caso de que*, (in case that), and *antes (de) que* (before) often trigger the subjunctive. Look at these examples:

para que (so that)
*Llegaré temprano para que **podamos** ver la película.*
I'll arrive early so that we (might) see the movie.

antes (de) que (before)
*Ricardo estudiaba antes de que **tomaran** el examen.*
Ricardo studied before they (probably) took the exam.

en caso (de) que (in case that)
*Voy a comprar un paraguas en caso de que **llueva**.*
I'm going to buy an umbrella in case that it (may) rain.

By the way, most "time-related" conjunctions that introduce an adverbial clause are followed by the subjunctive when the main clause includes a command: *Llámeme cuando se vayan.* (Call me whenever they leave.) or refers to future time: *Conversaremos hasta que termine el juego.* (We'll chat until whenever the game is over.)

¿Quieres Practicar?

Give the general idea of each of these sentences in English:

1. *Limpiaron todo antes de que llegara mi novia.*

2. *El gato vendrá cuando la señora lo llame.*

3. *Practiquen la canción hasta que la sepan.*

4. *Tomás contaba antes de que perdiera su dinero.*

5. *Trajo un sombrero en caso de que saliera sol.*

B. ADJECTIVE CLAUSES

An adjective clause modifies the noun. If the noun being modified in the main clause is unknown, uncertain, or nonexistent, the subjunctive is used. These are easy to recognize, because they're often introduced by the word *que* and followed by a verb:

Vamos a ver una película que me haga llorar.
(Let's see a movie that might make me cry.)

Quiero un empleado que hable español.
(I want an employee who may speak Spanish.)

The subjunctive is also used when the subject is unknown or when words such as *donde* or *quien* are in an adjective clause:

No hay ningún plato que le guste ordenar.
(There isn't a dish that he may want to order.)

Busco un lugar donde pueda nadar.
(I'm looking for a place where I might be able to swim.)

 ¡CONVERSEMOS!

Whenever you speak, do not confuse your audience! Use the subjunctive only to express DOUBT, DESIRES, EMOTION, DENIAL, and other INDEFINITE MESSAGES. Notice the difference between these two adjective clauses:

Necesita una casa que tiene garaje.
She needs a house that has a garage. (The speaker is sure that one exists)

Necesita una casa que tenga garaje.
She needs a house that (possibly) has a garage. (The speaker is unsure)

 ¡OYE!

Remember that the sequence of tenses is the same for adjective clauses and for adverbial and noun clauses (i.e., present → present):

Necesito un médico que hable español.
I need a doctor who (possibly) speaks Spanish.

Necesitaba un medico que hablara español.
I needed a doctor who (possibly) spoke Spanish.

No conozco a nadie que haya viajado a Chile.
I do not know anyone who might (possibly) have traveled to Chile.

¿Quieres Practicar?

Finish each sentence by creating your own adjective clause in the subjunctive:

1. *Mercedes busca un carro (tener _____).*

   Mercedes busca un carro que tenga cuatro puertas.

2. *Ellas querían un apartamento (estar cerca de _____).*

   _____

3. *Hablaré con una persona (hablar _____).*

   _____

4. *No había ninguna persona (saber usar _____).*

   _____

5. *Santiago quiere tomar las clases (ser más _____).*

   _____

THE VERB *GUSTAR*

me, te, le, nos, os, les

Words like *gustar* only have two forms that must agree with the subject: *gusta* (it is liked) and *gustan* (they are liked). You also need an indirect object before *gustar* to tell who relates to the thing being liked (by me, etc.). There's no matching construction in English, because the literal translation is reversed: *me* (by me) *gusta* (it is liked); *me* (by me) *gustan* (they are liked). Here's the simple meaning:

	MEANING		MEANING
me gusta	I like it	*nos gusta*	we like it
me gustan	I like them	*nos gustan*	we like them
te gusta	you like it (sing. inf.)	*os gusta*	you like it (pl. inf.)
te gustan	you like them (sing. inf.)	*os gustan*	you like them (pl. inf.)
le gusta	he, she likes it you like it (sing. form.)	*les gusta*	they like it you like it (pl. form.)
le gustan	he, she likes them you like them (sing. form.)	*les gustan*	they like them you like them (pl. form.)

These verbs act the same as *gustar*, so study the examples. Again, notice the simple meaning:

encantarle (to love something)	*Me encanta la música.* (I love the music.)
faltarle (to be missing something)	*Les faltan las llaves.* (They're missing the keys.)
importarle (to be important)	*¿Le importa el día?* (Is the day important to him?)
tocarle (to take one's turn)	*Te toca a ti.* (It's your turn.)
interesarle (to be interested)	*No nos interesan.* (We're not interested in them.)

Words like *gustar* also work well with verb infinitives, but you'll have to use the third person singular form. Add the (*a* + stressed pronoun) construction to clarify: *A ellos les gusta bailar la salsa.* (They like to dance salsa.) Here's the formula for using verbs like *gustar*:

A+ STRESSED PRONOUN	+ I.O. PRONOUN	+ *GUSTA(N)*	+ NOUN(S)/INFINTIVE
A	*ellos*	*les*	*gustan*	*los tacos*
A	*mi*	*me*	*gusta*	*cantar*

¡LEE Y ESCRIBE!

Indirect object pronouns are also used with some verbs to communicate special messages. For example, sometimes they are added to unusual *se* constructions that express mishaps or unplanned events:

caérsele (to drop)	*Se me cayó el vaso.*	I dropped the glass.
acabársele (to run out of)	*Se le acaba el dinero.*	He's running out of money.
perdérsele (to lose)	*Se nos perdió la cámara.*	We lost the camera.

¿Quieres Practicar?

Use the correct form of the special verb:

1. *A ella le __falta__ un cuaderno. (faltar)*

2. *Nos _____ veinte minutos. (quedar)*

3. *¿Te _____ verme mañana? (interesar)*

4. *A ellos les _____ viajar. (gustar)*

5. *¿No te _____ los resultados? (importar)*

2. *quedan*   3. *interesa*   4. *gusta*   5. *importan*

USING VERB INFINITIVES

In Spanish, you can say a lot simply by using verb infinitives in certain structures. For example, the infinitive is often used after conjugated verb forms to complement or complete the main idea in a sentence. Remember that the verb's tense will not affect the infinitive's meaning:

I. Verb + Infinitive

Queremos trabajar contigo. (We want to work with you.)

Deben volver a la una. (They should return at one o'clock.)

No sabía coser. (I didn't know how to sew.)

¿Puedes hacerlo? (Can you do it?)

Prefererería tomar el tren. (He'd prefer to take the train.)

¡OYE!

An infinitive is also used after verbs of sense perception, such as *oír*, *ver*, *sentir*, *mirar*, and *escuchar* to indicate a completed event or action. Notice the difference when a gerund ("-ing" word) is used instead:

Le oí cantar.	I heard him sing.
Le oí cantando.	I heard him (while he was) singing.
¿Me vieron salir?	Did you see me leave?
¿Me vieron saliendo?	Did you see me (as I was) leaving?

II. Verb + Preposition + Infinitive

Students get into trouble with some verb forms, because the infinitive construction also requires the preposition *a*, *de*, or *en*:

A

bajar a (to lower)	*Bajemos a comer.*	Let's go down(stairs) to eat.
subir a (to go up)	*Ha subido a dormir.*	He's gone upstairs to sleep.
comenzar a (to begin to)	*Comenzó a llover.*	It began to rain.

DE

acabar de (to have just)	*Acabamos de leerlo.*	We have just read it.
dejar de (to stop)	*Dejaron de gritar.*	They stopped yelling.
tratar de (to try to)	*No he tratado de entrar.*	I haven't tried to enter.

EN

pensar en (to think of)	*No pensé en eso.*	I didn't think about that.
insistir en (to insist upon)	*Insisto en pintarla.*	I insist on having it painted.
quedar en (to agree to)	*Han quedado en vender.*	They have agreed to sell.

> It won't be long now! Just be sure you're using all the
> tips and shortcuts as you learn this new material.

¡PALABRAS EXTRAS!

There are also a few verbs that require the preposition *con* before the infinitive. Here are some examples:

amenazar con (to threaten to)	*Amenazó con irse.* She threatened to leave.
contar con (to count on)	*Cuento contigo.* I'm counting on you.
soñar con (to dream about)	*Sueña con los angelitos.* Dream about little angels.

¿Quieres Practicar?

To complete the sentence, put one of the missing words (*a, de, en*) on each line below. If one is not needed, leave the line blank:

1. *Insistían __en__ no comprar un nuevo estereo.*

2. *Acaban _____ llegar.*

3. *Pensamos _____ hacerlo más tarde.*

4. *Quisiera _____ invitar a Susana.*

5. *Comenzamos _____ caminar.*

2. de   3. en   4.   5. a

III. Other Uses of the Infinitive

Verb infinitives are used frequently in Spanish, which eliminates the need for conjugations:

1. As <u>nouns</u>: *El **escribir** es importante.* (Writing is important.)
2. As <u>commands</u>: *No **correr**. Favor de **caminar**.* (No running. Please walk.)
3. As <u>casual expressions:</u> *¡A **estudiar**!* (Off to study!)
4. After <u>impersonal expressions</u>: *Es difícil **cortar** la carne.* (It's hard to cut meat.)
5. After many <u>prepositions</u>: *Lo hicimos para **ganar**.* (We did it in order to win.)
6. After a "<u>question word</u>": *¿Sabía qué **cocinar**?* (Did she know what to cook?)
7. After <u>que</u> in certain cases: *Tenían mucho que **hacer**.* (They had a lot to do.)
8. After <u>tener que</u>: *Tenemos que **viajar** mucho.* (We have to travel a lot.)
9. After <u>IR + A</u>: *Vamos a **salir**.* (We're going to leave.)

¡OYE!

When *ESTAR* is followed by *para* and an infinitive, it means "to be about to," but when *ESTAR* is followed by *por* and an infinitive, it means "to be in favor of":

Estoy para salir.   I'm about to leave.
Estoy por terminarlo.   I'm in favor of finishing it.

¿Quieres Practicar?

a.) Put the words in order in each of the following sentences. Remember that in Spanish there may be two or more ways to do so!

1. *bonito / para / busco / comprar / algo*   *Busco algo bonito para comprar.*

2. *la noche / sin / trabajaba / toda / dormir* _____

3. *que / nada / no / decirle / hay* _____

4. *el / es / música / para / tocar / piano* _____

5. *mucho / tenía / hacer / ella / que* _____

b.) Translate these sentences into Spanish the best way you know how:

1. It's possible to swim in the lake.   *Es posible nadar en el lago.*

2. The room is easy to paint. _____

3. We have to write these words. _____

4. They have many things to buy. _____

5. It's important to bring the books. _____

¡LEE Y ESCRIBE!

Notice how the object naturally follows the transitive verb's infinitive in this construction:

Es difícil   ver   la luna. (It's difficult to see the moon.)
          INFINITIVE   OBJECT

However, if the object (or clause) does not follow the infinitive of a transitive verb, the construction ADJECTIVE + *DE* + INFINITIVE is used:

La luna es   difícil de ver. (The moon is difficult to see.)
OBJECT   ADJ. + *DE* + INFINITIVE

¡CONVERSEMOS!

Here's another word used with infinitives that creates confusion. The meanings change entirely if you add a preposition in the case of *deber* (should) vs. *deber de* (must).

Ella <u>debe</u> llegar a la una. (She <u>should</u> arrive at one.)
Ella <u>debe de</u> llegar a la una. (She <u>must</u> arrive at one.)

REFLEXIVE VERBS

me, te, se, nos, os, se

I. Common Usage

Reflexive infinitives have *se* at the end and require a reflexive pronoun (*me, te, se, nos, os, se*) as part of its conjugated form. As a result, they are easy to recognize in any sentence:

Bañarse (to bathe oneself)

(yo)	**me baño**	I bathe myself
(tú)	**te bañas**	you bathe yourself (inf. sing.)
(él, ella, Ud.)	**se baña**	he bathes himself
		or she bathes herself
		or you bathe yourself (form. sing.)
(nosotros)	**nos bañamos**	we bathe ourselves
(vosotros)	**os bañáis**	you bathe yourselves (inf. pl.)
(ellos, ellas, Uds.)	**se bañan**	they bathe themselves
		or you bathe yourselves (form. pl.)

All it means when a verb is reflexive is that the action **remains with the subject**:

REFLEXIVE VERB	EXAMPLE
llamarse (to call oneself)	*El niño se llama Octavio.*
	(The boy calls himself Octavio.)
afeitarse (to shave oneself)	*Ellos se afeitan cada noche.*
	(They shave themselves every night.)
lavarse (to wash oneself)	*Siempre me lavo el pelo.*
	(I always wash my hair.)
ponerse (to put on)	*Nos pusimos los zapatos.*
	(We put on our shoes.)
quebrarse (to get broken)	*No se quebró la pierna.*
	(He didn't break his leg.)
despertarse (to awaken)	*¿A qué hora se despertó?*
	(What time did he wake up?)

Remember that the reflexive pronoun is often attached to the end of the verb in affirmative commands: *Vístete.* (Get dressed.), infinitives: *Quiere vestirse.* (He wants to get dressed.), and present participles: *Estoy vistiéndome.* (I'm getting dressed.)

¡PALABRAS EXTRAS!

Watch it! Just because a verb has *se* at the end doesn't mean it has to be reflexive. Several Spanish verbs have reflexive forms, but do not have reflexive meanings. The following verbs exist exclusively in the reflexive:

acordarse	to remember	*arrepentirse*	to repent
atreverse a	to dare	*desmayarse*	to faint
divorciarse	to divorce	*jactarse*	to boast

¿Quieres Practicar?

a.) *¿Qué hace la gente cada mañana?* Follow the model given:

1. *despertarse*   _Se despiertan._

2. *bañarse* _____

3. *lavarse los dientes* _____

4. *peinarse* _____

5. *ponerse la ropa* _____

b.) Fill in the blanks with the correct present tense form of the reflexive verb:

1. *Juan (quitarse) la camisa y (ponerse) una limpia.*   _se quita, se pone_

2. *Los niños (lavarse) las manos con agua y jabón.* _____

3. *¿Cómo (vestirse) el Sr. Martínez?* _____

4. *Trabajamos todo el día y (acostarse) temprano.* _____

5. *No (venderse) licor en esa tienda.* _____

3. *Se lavan los dientes*   4. *Se peinan*   5. *Se ponen la ropa*   3. *se viste*   5. *se vende*
2. *Se bañan*   2. *se lavan*   4. *nos acostamos*

¡OYE!

With reference to things, reflexive verbs generally express "by itself" or "by themselves":

Se cerraron las puertas.   The doors closed (by themselves).

II. Other Uses

A. RECIPROCAL. Reflexive verbs in their plural form may express reciprocal action, which is usually clarified by the context: *Pepe y Linda se quieren mucho.* (Carlos and Linda love each other a lot.), *Nos conocimos hace años.* (We met years ago.)

B. INDEFINITE. These indefinite constructions in English are expressed by the third person reflexive in Spanish, and may be translated in a variety of ways: *¿Cómo se escribe la palabra?* (How does one write the word?), *Aquí se habla español.* (Spanish is spoken here.)

C. IDIOMS. Several reflexive verbs are considered to be idiomatic expressions: *Nos pusimos de acuerdo.* (We came to an agreement.), *Ella nunca se da por vencida.* (She never gives up.), *Me hice daño.* (I hurt myself.), *Todos se hicieron médicos.* (They all became doctors.), *La vecina se volverá loca.* (The neighbor will go crazy.)

¡SECRETOS!

The Hispanic culture is full of reflexives, which gives it more of a poetic flavor. Spanish even has unique reflexive expressions that need to be studied separately. For example, *OLVIDARSE* uses an indirect object pronoun, while *OLVIDARSE (DE)* does not:

Se le olvidó el nombre.

Se olvidó del nombre.

} He forgot the name.

Another example is *EQUIVOCARSE*, which means "to be wrong" only when the subject is a person:

Te equivocas si piensas que voy a pagar la cuenta.
You are wrong if you think I'm going to pay this bill.

¿Quieres Practicar?

Answer these questions about yourself in complete sentences:

1. *¿A qué hora se despierta Ud.?*
2. *¿Se desayuna Ud. con su familia?*
3. *¿A Ud. le gusta ponerse ropa nueva?*
4. *¿Se cansa mucho Ud. con sus estudios?*
5. *¿Cuántas veces por semana se reúne Ud. con sus amigos?*

THE PASSIVE VOICE

ser + **Past Participle** + *por*

In both Spanish and English, there is an active voice in which the subject does the acting, and a passive voice in which the subject is acted upon by an "agent" or doer of the action. The passive voice in Spanish is formed with the verb **SER** + **PAST PARTICIPLE** + **POR** construction:

ACTIVE

Ellos sirvieron el desayuno.
They served breakfast.

PASSIVE

El desayuno **fue servido por** *ellos.*
Breakfast was served by them.

In the passive voice, the past participle and the subject must agree in number and gender. All tenses of the verb **SER** are conjugated normally, although the verb is in the preterit when referring to past time:

Los documentos fueron recibidos por el funcionario.
The documents were received by the government official.

 ### *¿Quieres Practicar?*

Change these sentences from the active voice to the passive:

1. *El autor escribió un nuevo libro.*

    <u>El nuevo libro fue escrito por el autor.</u>

2. *Nosotros hemos cambiado el número.*

    _____

3. *El cartero ha perdido la carta.*

    _____

4. *Ellas preparan la comida.*

    _____

5. *La vecina cerró las ventanas.*

    _____

5. *Las ventanas fueron cerradas por la vecina.*
4. *La comida fue preparada por ellas.*
3. *La carta ha sido perdida por el cartero.*
2. *El número ha sido cambiado por nosotros.*

¡LEE Y ESCRIBE!

The "true" passive is considered somewhat more formal, and is used more often in literature than in everyday speech.

HOW TO GET AN A+

We have found in this chapter that there are a few areas of Spanish that consistently create problems for students, so we needed to study them separately. They include the **subjunctive mood**, **verb infinitives**, **reflexive verbs**, **verbs like *gustar***, and the **passive voice**. Master these along with the basics, and there's not much else you'll need to worry about. However, the real key to getting an A+ in Spanish is having the ability to communicate without concern, which only comes from daily review and practice. Let's close our training with suggestions on how to internalize what you have learned so far.

Chapter 8
Capítulo Ocho

Let's Review
Vamos a Repasar

The emphasis in this chapter is on Spanish skills review, and it includes a variety of helpful discussion topics. Read each section carefully, write down anything that you may find helpful, and consider rereading this entire chapter when you're done!

BE PREPARED

Perhaps the most important skill for every Spanish student is preparation, which is the ability to make sure everything is in order before the actual class begins. Skillful students are able to evaluate the entire program beforehand, as well as overcome any personal fears they may have about learning a new language. Studying a foreign language is a difficult task, and not everyone knows the steps that must be taken in order to have success. Here's a closer look at prepping for the language-learning experience:

BE PREPARED: LEARNING IN THE RIGHT ENVIRONMENT

When it comes to acquiring any new skill, people seldom consider the importance of maintaining the appropriate learning environment. This is particularly true for Spanish students, since where you learn a foreign language often determines how fast you will actually learn it. For those who study in a classroom environment, this phenomenon is quite obvious. Whether it's large or small group instruction or even one-on-one training, Spanish students seem to learn more when they like their learning environment. Interestingly, the same holds true for those who study outside the classroom. No matter where you decide to learn Spanish—in public or in private—your immediate surroundings must be considered carefully prior to studying new language skills.

Anyone can pick up a foreign language in a classroom once they feel comfortable enough to do so. So, what's the problem? Though there are other factors, many students don't learn because they suffer from something called situational anxiety, which is a feeling of intense stress within a certain environment. For example, most beginning Spanish students experience strong negative feelings the moment they enter the classroom. This then leads to a reluctance to focus or participate, especially when other students in the class appear to be more proficient in the language.

The best remedy for such anxiety is self-awareness, which means that you must identify those personal feelings that could be causing the concern. You need to ask yourself, "Am I stressed out because I don't feel accepted and liked?" "Am I doubtful because I'm not sure I can learn?" "Am I upset because I don't like the teacher or classroom setting?" Such feelings are entirely normal, since the traditional foreign language classroom is well-known for its unfriendly confines that often lead to embarrassment, bewilderment, and not much success.

Once you become aware of your feelings, it is then possible to accept your situational anxiety as merely part of the learning process. This acceptance will help you gain self-confidence, which is needed as you evaluate the place where you intend to study. And, what makes a location more appealing and conducive to acquiring a foreign language? Basically, there are five key elements to look for, and they can be noted immediately. These are also helpful recommendations that you can make to your Spanish instructor:

1. The arrangement of desks, chairs, and tables must allow for lots of personal interaction, not only between students and teacher but also among individual students.

2. Every student must have a good view of what's going on during the language lesson, in order to eliminate frustration, disinterest, or confusion.

3. Students need a large open space in the room for group activities, such as a play, musical performance, or other live presentation.

4. Room decor must be colorful, busy, and fun.

5. The acoustics in the room must allow for softly spoken words to be projected from one end of the room to the other.

Although it may seem unusual to discuss such matters with a classroom teacher, it is still worth a try. The fact of the matter is learning does improve when students are taught in the appropriate setting. You will find that many Spanish instructors will actually listen to their students and make changes in order to improve the classroom environment.

But, not everyone studies Spanish in a traditional classroom. A growing number of students have made the choice to learn new language skills on their own, without the benefits of real-life instruction. Interactive webinars, downloadable applications, online programs, and CD or DVD tools now allow learners to sit just about anywhere with a portable device and study a foreign language.

Surprisingly, these independent students must also maintain an appropriate learning environment in order for them to find success. Poor lighting, interruptions, stuffiness, background noise, room temperature, and other distractions can ruin a Spanish lesson, yet are common occurrences when studying at home, work, or in a public setting. As a result, individual students must take certain measures to secure the best learning atmosphere possible prior to studying language outside the classroom. Steps include finding an isolated spot away from crowds and disturbances, turning off the cell phone, making sure the computer works properly, and knowing the limitations of one's own language program.

It is also important to maintain a consistent learning environment, instead of frequently changing locations. By establishing a specific place for language study, learners feel more secure and comfortable about using new skills. Obviously, the ideal situation for anyone who wants to pick up Spanish is to receive live instruction in a motivational classroom, alongside other students who are eager to learn.

¡OYE!

Try not to study Spanish for extended periods of time. Language sessions should never drive students to exhaustion, frustration, or boredom. Make sure you know precisely how much language you can personally absorb at one sitting. Set limits for yourself, even in a classroom setting. Otherwise, you'll end up feeling overwhelmed, which is the first step toward dropping out completely. Simply remember that learning Spanish takes time, so you'll need to be patient with yourself. Take short breaks when you begin to feel besieged by too much information. You can only learn Spanish when your mind is alert, refreshed, and willing to concentrate.

BE PREPARED: EVALUATING YOUR INSTRUCTOR

Having the ideal learning environment is not the only key to becoming a better Spanish student. Much of the responsibility belongs to the instructor, and this includes any online or digital trainer who is assigned to teach you language. This means that once you have scoped out and improved your surroundings, you must immediately begin to evaluate your teacher. Perhaps the best way to do this is by moving through a checklist of "Qualities of a Great Spanish Teacher," which can help assess how effective your instruction might be. Spend some time grading him or her by using this five-point scale, so that you can evaluate your Spanish teacher fairly:

QUALITIES OF A GREAT SPANISH TEACHER
Evaluation Form

1 = Excellent   2 = Good   3 = Average   4 = Poor   5 = Very Poor

SCORE   PERSONAL TRAITS

_____   Pleasant to watch or look at

_____   Articulate and clear

_____   Personable and friendly

_____   Animated or expressive

_____   Humorous or clownish

_____   Excited or motivated

_____   Patient or controlled

_____   Positive or complimentary

_____   Validating or supportive

_____   Skilled and knowledgeable

_____   Sensitive or tactful

SCORE   CLASS MANAGEMENT SKILLS

_____   Builds student self-confidence

_____   Creates a stress-free atmosphere

_____   Promotes a collaborative spirit

_____   Provides clear directions

_____   Assists students in need

_____   Senses student discomfort or confusion

_____   Makes good eye contact

_____   Encourages questions and risk-taking

_____   Learns student names quickly

_____   Takes interest in personal lives of students

_____   Keeps classroom activity in order

_____   Supplies students with necessary materials

_____   Motivates students continuously

SCORE   CLASS INSTRUCTION SKILLS

_____   Pronounces words clearly

_____   Writes legibly

_____   Allows for speaking errors

_____   Repeats frequently

_____   Prepares well for each lesson

_____   Understands and speaks English well

_____   Adds gestures when speaking Spanish

_____   Avoids boring practice exercises

_____   Mixes guided drills with communicative activities

_____   Begins and closes with review

_____   Provides for a warm-up period

_____   Teaches vocabulary with real-life objects

_____   Shows lots of pictures or video clips

_____   Uses a variety of written materials

_____   Assigns in-class and take-home interviews

_____   Labels items with stickers or name cards

_____   Plays music during class time

_____   Stresses cultural understanding

_____   Incorporates listening, speaking, reading, and writing practice

_____   Makes learning Spanish fun

Although this form is incomplete, it is still a great tool for any foreign language student. It paints a detailed picture of the ideal Spanish instructor. Completing an evaluation like this is essential, because once you know "how" you will be taught you can make the necessary adjustments.

On the average, today's Spanish teachers score very well; however, that may not always be the case. This may result in either meeting with the teacher privately to discuss concerns or withdrawing from the class altogether. Unfortunately, most students skip this step in the process. They tend to enter a Spanish program believing that as long as the teacher has some knowledge and experience, everyone should be able to learn.

¡OYE!

Any teaching activity that creates frustration, such as traditional grammar-based language learning, can negatively impact the Spanish student. In a natural learning environment, the main task of the teacher is to encourage each learner to become more independent and experimental, rather than to impose additional tasks or explanations.

BE PREPARED: UNDERSTANDING YOUR TEXTBOOK

Once you have secured a place to study and successfully evaluated your instructor, why not take a look at the Spanish program itself. Even if you have been assured time and again that you are in the best course available, remember that not everyone learns language the same. This is also true for Spanish textbooks. What clearly appeals to some could be soundly rejected by others.

As a result, be sure to examine your Spanish program closely, which includes doing some research on the Internet. Find out what others are saying about your textbook. Learn about other Spanish programs and compare. Most comprehensive Spanish programs include the following basic components, along with a teacher's guide, although several are beginning to add more engaging media, such as video clips, music, and online interaction. Some of these components are either combined or embedded into the primary textbook or packaged and sold separately:

Textbook (Language units and thematic lessons)
Workbook (Practice drills and exercises)
Dictionary or Glossary (Reference tools)
Tests (Assessments with answers)
Audio/Video Interactive CD/Online Tool (Listening/viewing with response)

Generally speaking, Spanish programs are divided into a series of language levels, although the focus of each level may differ depending upon the philosophy of the program's publisher. In other words, no two programs are exactly alike. However, although they may differ in format and presentation, there are still some similarities. Here's what you will probably discover:

- Dialogues, stories, graphics, or other methods are used to present thematic lessons.
- Grammar lessons are followed by practice exercises.
- Vocabulary is introduced in context within the lesson.
- Learning a lesson involves studying, memorizing, and preparing for tests.
- Lessons include communicative listening, speaking, reading, and writing practice.
- Cultural insights are introduced within the lessons.

Spanish lessons are supposed to build upon previously introduced material, so a good textbook always incorporates some chapter review. There should also be some logical transition from one lesson to the next. For example, some of the words and grammatical structures presented in the first chapter should also be found in chapter two. The secret is not to be overwhelmed by all the practice activities and language exercises. Very seldom will all of them be assigned.

The actual textbook pages should be evaluated, too. For example, reading is easier when the font size is legible, graphics are clear, and the pages do not appear cluttered. Remember that you'll be studying in that textbook for extended periods of time, so you may have to make some adjustments. If reading is strenuous, for instance, you might need to take more breaks during your study time. Also, if the textbook feels heavy, but has a soft cover, extra care will be needed as you carry it around. And, check page thickness, particularly if you like to highlight, create folds, or take notes in your Spanish book. Unfortunately, many textbooks today are not designed to handle normal wear and tear.

Once you receive your textbook, skim through it cover to cover. A typical unit, chapter, or lesson title in the book might be written in Spanish, so be sure to learn its translation. Generally, every chapter covers the following topics of interest, although not necessarily in this particular order:

Grammar rules (i.e., *Reglas gramaticales*)
Dialogues or readings (i.e., *Lenguaje práctico*)
Communicative activities (i.e., *Estrategias comunicativas*)
Thematic vocabulary (i.e., *Vocabulario necesario*)
Cultural insights (i.e., *La cultura latina*)
Open-ended discussions (i.e., *Temas para discutir*)

Don't forget that the heart of your Spanish program is the textbook, since everything else is essentially launched from there. The workbook, audio practice CD, and reference material are all built around the book's language lessons. Therefore, you'll need to read and reread each page of your textbook well.

¡OYE!

In terms of sitting down to read or study, be aware that where you sit and how you sit are both important. Before opening the book, find a comfortable chair with strong back support that allows you to rest both feet flat on the floor. Ideally, your chair should have armrests and cushioning. After you are comfortably seated, check your posture. Try to keep your knees at the same height as your hips and try not to cross your legs. Scoot back in your seat, so that your back is firmly against the chair back. Make sure your upper back and neck are straight, but still in a comfortable position. Relax your shoulders; don't pull them back or hunch them forward. Pick up your book and tilt it up toward you. Hold it close enough to your eyes so that you do not have to strain your vision. Take ample breaks and avoid sitting in one position for long periods of time. And, don't forget your body is designed to move frequently, so try not to sit all day reading Spanish books!

BE PREPARED: PRACTICING WITHOUT FEAR

As a rule, there are two basic aspects of fear when it comes to learning Spanish. The first aspect takes place within the classroom and encompasses fears related to the unknown and fears of academic failure. Such fears are quite normal and usually dissipate once the course is under way. The second aspect of fear, which is based on the fear of failure, is more complex, because it is linked to practicing the language with people who speak Spanish fluently. This is especially true for beginning students, who often ask:

Will I accidently say something rude, hurtful, or offensive?
Will I look or sound like a complete fool?
Will I be corrected, teased, or laughed at by others?
Will I forget what I want to say and be stuck in silence?
Will I somehow create a major scandal?

The troubling thing is that according to experts, learning Spanish is supposed to be fun, not an experience rocked by fear! Evidently, when students pick it up naturally, like children do with their first language, all the fears and pressures seem to fade away. Kids in a sandbox can learn no matter how many languages there are, simply because they tend to play with their communication skills until they get it right. Surprisingly, that's also the way older students like you are designed to learn—by having a good time—naturally.

Nevertheless, studying grammar rules, completing exercises, memorizing vocabulary, and taking tests are still procedures in any valid Spanish program. Unfortunately, most people are afraid to study Spanish because of them. The interesting thing is that the human brain actually enjoys the work! As long as things are explained clearly and made relevant, there's nothing that should stop a child, teen, or adult from learning more. You need to realize there's no reason to fear speaking Spanish at all. Here are the facts:

- Spanish grammar and pronunciation improve the more you practice through trial and error.
- Personal communication is always more important than conjugation. The fact that you are even trying to speak Spanish will motivate Latinos to help you along.
- If Spanish speakers try to respond back to you in English instead of Spanish, they are not being critical: they just want to try out their own English skills.
- People with a lighthearted, outgoing, childlike approach seem to pick up Spanish faster than others. They appear to overcome shyness, swallow their pride, and just go for it.
- When Latinos giggle as you speak, they're enjoying themselves and the experience. Your mistakes may sound funny to them, so feel free to join in the laughter.
- Humiliation in class and embarrassment in public are never fun, but they are not that serious when caused by language errors. Embrace the fact that you'll need plenty of healthy self-esteem if you want to learn Spanish well.

So, do not be overwhelmed by fear! Make an honest confession to yourself that you are not a fluent native speaker, and that you will probably speak with language errors. Mistakes are inevitable with learning, and the worst mistake you could make would be to be fearful of using what you know. Remember that no matter how many mistakes you make, wherever you go in the Spanish-speaking world, your sincere attempts to learn the language will almost always be appreciated.

BE PREPARED: MAKING THE BIG COMMITMENT

Learning a foreign language is not an easy task, and it will take a huge commitment from you even to become somewhat proficient in Spanish. It would be ideal if there were a quick-fix learning method available, but unfortunately, the process is often-times a difficult one. Some studies suggest that real communication in another language comes after five years of arduous study, while others claim that under the right conditions it can be picked up much sooner. There is even debate over identifying the optimal age or personality type for learning Spanish. Regardless of these factors, however, any individual who intends to become fluent in a foreign language will truly have to work for it.

In order to keep such a commitment, there are certain measures that need to be taken. The most notable involves scheduling, which means that you must organize your daily activities so that they include some Spanish study and practice time. This also means that you have to attend class regularly. To get an A+ in Spanish, learners must commit to taking the complete course and participating as much as possible. Here's a sample student schedule for a typical Monday–Wednesday class. Notice that each day differs slightly and that some actions are not really Spanish assignments. For example, playing a Spanish-language music CD, watching Spanish TV, or playing a Spanish video game are all extracurricular activities, yet are still considered effective ways to learn another language:

Monday	**Tuesday**	**Wednesday**	**Thursday**	**Friday**
Music CD	*Music CD*	*Music CD*	*Music CD*	*Music CD*
CLASS	*Homework*	*CLASS*	*Language lab*	*Online game*
Vocab. list	*Study for quiz*	*Live practice*	*Short story*	*Spanish TV*

Besides scheduling, another step you can take is to work on your self-motivation. This involves rewarding yourself for any language learning successes or accomplishments. This may mean eating your favorite snack after completing a tough Spanish homework assignment or perhaps buying a music download if you score high on a test. Motivation is the primary force behind learning, so you should always take time out to recognize and praise your own language growth.

Still another step toward making the commitment to learning Spanish is securing outside support. Since it takes years to develop good communication skills, you will need family, teachers, and friends to encourage you along the way. You can also benefit from the help of a personal tutor or an enthusiastic group of fellow learners, in order to overcome barriers to fluency. Securing loyal supporters, like staying motivated, is an essential key to getting an A+ in Spanish. In fact, the more people you have in your life that are willing to champion your efforts, the sooner you will acquire the language.

Another secret to staying committed is making sure you know exactly what your ultimate goal is. Though you may take measures to stay on course, questions about your final objective might still remain. "What will I do with the Spanish I'm learning?" "How far do I plan to go?" "Why am I taking Spanish anyway?" These are all legitimate concerns that help determine one's commitment level. Once you know what you are shooting for, the job will become a lot less stressful. Also, be sure to ask yourself how much you really enjoy the Spanish language. Students need to like the language they are learning and at least some aspects of its culture if they plan on studying it for awhile.

One final area of commitment for Spanish students is time spent on the Internet, simply because the Internet now offers a wide range of content and learning materials. There are numerous free or low-cost websites with excellent learning tools, apps, online tutors, and even access to folks from Spanish-speaking countries with whom you can speak and interact. The Internet is a virtual classroom, library, bookstore, language laboratory, and support community. It is the home of the language-learning revolution, and now, with our advances in technology, the Internet is available wherever and whenever we want it, at no or very little cost.

Without question, learning Spanish takes plenty of self-discipline and personal sacrifice. Scheduling, finding ways to stay motivated, seeking support, setting goals, and spending time on the Internet are all required if you truly are committed to getting an A+ in Spanish.

¡OYE!

Although studying Spanish does not have to be expensive, learners tend to invest in these:

Tutoring sessions	Spanish TV or satellite channels
Spanish apps	Handheld devices, e-readers, etc.
Online help or support materials	International cell phone or Skype minutes
Language books and audio CDs	Travel expenses to Latin America

WHERE STUDENTS GO WRONG

As with any other skill, learning Spanish has certain barriers that all students must overcome in order to find success. These barriers are nothing more than annoying pitfalls that most English-speaking students seem to fall into time and again along the pathway to fluency. Once you can identify the pitfalls and know how to deal with them, learning Spanish will accelerate and not be as challenging as before.

The first pitfall is actually a mindset or way of thinking, and is probably the most dangerous pitfall of all. Almost all Spanish students have moments when they sense the enormity of learning a new language and begin to feel anxious. The problem arises when these feelings lead to thoughts of discouragement, frustration, or even self-doubt. Questions arise, such as, "Is this really worth all the hard work and commitment?" "How effective is this language program anyway?" or "Am I ever going to learn Spanish well?" You may even compare yourself to others, become pessimistic, and then refuse to join in. Or, you may become unenthusiastic about your learning environment, teacher, or materials, and then want to quit. Whatever the reason, these negative thoughts are very destructive and can drive anyone away from studying a second language.

By and large, this mindset is based on either unpleasant experiences or harmful misinformation. When you have failed at learning in the past and believe that you will probably be unsuccessful now, it is difficult to stay motivated. The problem is then compounded by all the negative commentaries out there that relate to learning Spanish, which are for the most part inaccurate, incomplete, and even inappropriate. Moreover, many so-called experts claim that certain programs, books, or other learning tools are superior to their competition, which often leads to a never-ending search for the "perfect" Spanish course. Worse yet, some get fooled by an advertisement, so they end up purchasing a product that is not even close to what was originally promised. No wonder so many learners are downbeat, dissatisfied, and want to walk away!

So, avoid this major pitfall by being aware of what you're thinking. Stop and ask yourself if your thoughts are in a positive or negative mode. Then, motivate yourself to focus on what you've learned so far. Believe that you can learn more, even if it's a little at a time. And never forget—your brain is learning Spanish in spite of your disappointment. According to science, as long as your textbook is open and Spanish is being spoken around you, the language is being stored within your mind.

As for the other student pitfalls, they refer to learning certain Spanish skills and are much easier to handle. In fact, if you review the following list on a regular basis, you will be much further along in the language-learning process than everyone else:

LISTENING AND SPEAKING SKILLS
- Confusing the vowel sounds, such as hearing the *i* and thinking it's an *e*.
- Confusing the consonant sounds, such as hearing the *j* sound and thinking it's an *h*.
- Pronouncing words with *rr* without rolling the r's, such as saying *caro* (expensive) instead of *carro* (car).
- Pronouncing words with *ll* as if it were *l*, such as saying *polo* (shirt) instead of *pollo* (chicken).
- Pronouncing words with *ñ* as if they were *n*, such as saying *ano* (anus) instead of *año* (year).
- Mispronouncing words due to not understanding accentuation, such as saying *esta* instead of *está*.
- Pronouncing the *h* in Spanish, although it is a silent letter.
- Forgetting that the *z* is pronounced as an *s* in Spanish.
- Forgetting that the *v* is pronounced more like a *b* in Spanish.
- Translating literally, such as saying *Estoy frío.* instead of *Tengo frío.* (I'm cold.)
- Getting the gender of nouns mixed up, such as incorrectly saying *la problema* instead of *el problema*.

- Forgetting to reverse the order of adjectives and nouns in a sentence, such as saying *grande casa* instead of *casa grande*.
- Inserting *por* instead of *para* after assuming that *por* always means "for," and saying *Es por usted.* instead of *Es para usted.* (It's for you.)
- Distinguishing between the informal *tú* and the formal *usted* forms, such as addressing a stranger with *¿Cómo estás tú?* instead of *¿Cómo está usted?* (How are you?)
- Using Spanish slang, street language, or curse words without knowing what the words really mean.

READING AND WRITING SKILLS

- Forgetting to write accent marks on words that require them, such as with *sí* and *cómo*.
- Spelling words as if they were in English, such as writing *impossible* instead of *imposible*.
- Forgetting to apply a double negative, such as writing *Hay nadie.* instead of *No hay nadie.* to express "There is no one."
- Guessing incorrectly at cognate word translations, such as reading *sopa* (soup) and thinking it means "soap."
- Overusing the subject pronouns, such as constantly adding *yo* (I) before verbs in a sentence even when it's already understood who's doing the talking.
- Mixing up the verbs *ser* and *estar*, such as writing *Estoy estudiante.* instead of *Soy estudiante.* (I am a student.)
- Forgetting proper use of prepositions, such as writing *en la mañana* instead *de la mañana* (in the morning).
- Making capitalization errors, such as putting capitals on the days of the week.
- Dropping the article on the days of the week, such as writing *Trabajo lunes*, instead of *Trabajo el lunes*.
- Using *se* and the reflexive verbs incorrectly, such as writing *Se fue al banco.* instead of *Fue al banco.* (He went to the bank.)
- Applying regular verb conjugations upon irregular verbs, such as writing *sabo* instead of *sé* (I know).
- Forgetting to use indirect object pronouns, such as *le* in *Le dí el dinero al Juan.* (I gave the money to John.)
- Getting the preterit and imperfect tenses confused, such as writing *Trabajé toda la noche.* instead of *Trabajaba toda la noche.* (I worked all night.)
- Forgetting irregular verb rules, such as those dealing with spelling changes and stem changes.
- Spending too little time learning how to use verbs in the subjunctive mood.

PRACTICE ACTIVITIES

Obviously, the best way to fix one's errors includes the assistance of a fluent Spanish speaker. If that's not possible, then seriously commit to some, if not all, of the following practice activities:

I. Listen to Spanish as often as you can by way of:

- Audio CDs or clips
- DVDs or video downloads
- Radio, TV, satellite programs
- Language-learning applications or products
- Any Spanish interactive website, podcast, or online tool with sound
- Participation in real-life conversations in the target language—live or on the Internet

II. Experiment with Spanish where you can also have some fun:

- Participate in activities where you can learn Spanish lyrics and sing along
- Take a class in Latin dance where you'll be exposed to cultural interaction
- Consider attending any event or activity where Spanish will be spoken in a social setting, such as holiday celebrations, sports competitions, family parties, community gatherings, festivals, shows, and concerts

III. Use the "label and command" method, especially around the home. Place removable labels on objects, with their Spanish names in clear sight. Then, have someone command you in Spanish to find, touch, lift, look at, or move whatever it is you've labeled!

IV. Interview fluent Spanish speakers by asking a variety of non-threatening questions in Spanish and using different verb tenses. Meet regularly, and fill in their responses to your homemade questionnaire.

V. Create differently colored flashcards in order to remember the meanings and conjugations of Spanish verbs. Start off with white cards for regular verbs. Then try brightly colored cards for those pesky irregular ones. They even make ultra-bright cards, which work great for those awkward subjunctives and commands.

VI. Gather all the Spanish reading materials you can and see if you can guess at what they are trying to say. Leaflets, advertisements, and brochures are readily available, and many Spanish language websites have a home page that is easy to understand.

VII. No matter what your age, games are incredible teaching tools. Shop around or search the Internet for any language-learning games in Spanish. Concentration, Bingo, crosswords, and word search puzzles are the easiest kinds to begin with. Start with those designed for kids. Once you master the simpler games, move on to those activities that are geared for teens and adults.

VIII. Take note of all the "language" shortcuts or patterns you can find in Spanish, such as:

- The imperfect only has three irregulars: *ser*, *ver*, and *ir*.
- Most verbs ending in *-cer* or *-cir* have *-zc* in their forms.
- Irregular preterit forms end in the same letters, except for *dar*, *ser*, and *ir*.
- The *-n* ending on a verb form indicates "they" or "you (plural)."
- The *-mos* ending at the end of a verb form means "we" are involved.
- The *-o* ending in the present tense means "I" am involved.
- The *ó* ending in the preterit means "you, he, she, or it" is involved.
- *Tú* forms in the present tense end in *-s*, and *-ste* in the preterit.
- Relexive verbs conjugate normally but require *me*, *nos*, *te*, or *se* in front.
- The two most common two-part tenses are the present progressive and present perfect.
- The simple present tense has the most irregular changes, primarily in the 1st person singular form
- The present, preterit, and imperfect endings for regular verbs are all fairly consistent.

PRACTICE ACTIVITIES: SOME STUDENT SUGGESTIONS

Some of the best practice suggestions come from students like yourselves. Comments like these are found all over the Internet:

- "I'm a visual learner, so I spend at least a half hour every day watching Spanish TV or movies, sometimes online."
- "One method that works for me is to memorize small phrases. For example: *Tengo que ir . . .* (I have to go . . .). You can then plug in different words to that phrase to make completely different sentences: *Tengo que ir al baño.* (I have to go to the bathroom.), *Tengo que ir a clase.* (I have to go to class.)"
- "Always look or listen for the root of a Spanish word. For example, if you know that *pintar* means 'to paint,' you can easily guess at the meanings of *pintando, pintado, pintura, pintoresco*, etc."
- "There's nothing better than using flash cards, flash cards, and more flash cards!"
- "When learning the language, try listening to radio and Spanish TV, do some reading, and watch others speak. Staying relaxed will eventually do the trick."
- "Have conversations with yourself, either in your mind or out loud, so you don't feel the pressure to be correct. A good source of material is any conversation you recently had in English."
- "I used to practice Spanish with my cat or dog. They are good listeners and don't care how many mistakes you make!"

- "To me, I can't learn unless I really go for it, so I'm on the street downtown where lots of Spanish speakers go. I ask questions or try to chat, and everyone tries to help me. I'm learning faster than anyone in my class. Friendly conversations help best. You can even go to this club I know where they have amazing food and music. My friends think I'm crazy, and tell me I'm becoming more Latino, *pero me encanta la idea.*"

- "Try narrating your day aloud, telling what's going on in Spanish. If you don't know a word or how to express an idea in Spanish, just substitute it with English. Make it a game and try to have as little English in your narratives as possible. Eventually you'll be able to express just about anything in Spanish."

- "I'm always on free Spanish websites. There are dozens of them. Games and puzzles work great, but I also like pages that have free audio clips of native speakers saying words or phrases."

- "You'll lose it if you don't use it, so it's a matter of time with practice. Keep working at it, but always be ready to laugh at yourself when you're wrong!"

- "I like to translate what I hear or read, and it may not always be correct, but it gets me thinking in the language."

- "Try using a string of words you know, and eventually it will come out correctly. Also try greeting your friends and family in both Spanish and English. You can even try the same approach with Spanish speakers. People everywhere think it's great when you say things in two languages."

- "Immerse yourself in Spanish for a little while by listening to a podcast, watching a movie, or reading something, and then practice by chatting online, talking to yourself, writing, or doing anything that you find fun to do. I find it much easier to recall words and phrases in Spanish if I've just been absorbing it."

- "Try to dwell on maintaining a positive outlook. Positive emotions energize the brain, and increase the efficiency of learning. So, find things to read, watch, or listen to that are upbeat and optimistic. Pessimistic input and negative tension only decrease learning efficiency. You'll need to avoid a gloomy mindset at all costs!"

MORE SECRETS TO SUCCESS

Here are some things you should consider the next time you have doubts about getting an A+ in Spanish:

- Learning Spanish is painless! Unlike most other languages, thousands of Spanish words are spelled the same in English or are very similar!

- Learning Spanish is simple! Most Spanish speakers use simple vocabulary and verb forms to communicate, and they also tend to repeat the same basic words over and over again!

- Learning Spanish is practical! Millions of Latinos in the U.S. and Mexico speak some "Spanglish," a mixture of English and Spanish, so now hundreds of new words are easier to understand!
- Learning Spanish is valuable! Don't forget that bilingual employees are in high demand and the pay is generally higher!
- Learning Spanish is beneficial! Research suggests that people who know two languages are basically smarter than those with only one!
- Learning Spanish is fun! Knowing a foreign language can lead to new friendships and exciting cultural experiences!

And here are more helpful suggestions:

- Don't worry if you can understand what other people are saying in Spanish, but are too reluctant to speak. Believe me—if you're out there listening to the language regularly, your speech in Spanish will surface naturally whenever it's ready to.
- If you aren't fluent in Spanish after reading this book or taking a language course, don't fret. It takes years of continuous exposure and practice before you'll speak like a native.
- Feeling comfortable around people from Spanish-speaking countries will make a difference! The more you know about the Hispanic culture, the closer you'll be to understanding their language. It's also wise to study a map of Spain and Latin America.
- If you struggle with self-confidence, try to unwind before you say anything. Apply any stress-relief or relaxation techniques prior to conversing in Spanish. Take a deep breath, giggle, and then just go for it.
- Assertive, outgoing students usually pick up Spanish faster than others. So, try to guess, take chances, and experiment whenever you are unsure. A carefree attitude wins over an overly careful one.
- Courtesy is king in Spanish. The more respectful you are, the more Spanish you'll learn. So practice polite words and phrases every day, and as always, be friendly, patient, and sincere.
- Commit to practicing Spanish every single day—without fail. Whether it's searching online, trying a new greeting, or calling out items throughout the house, try to review and improve every chance you get!
- Bear in mind that being close in grammar and pronunciation is usually good enough. Folks will understand you as long as the key words are there, so avoid stopping to translate every little detail during a conversation. Roll with the general idea, and assess the damage later.
- Stop thinking about how much more you still need to learn. Hang out with other students who are similar to you in skills level, but are motivated and excited to learn more.

- Act like an A+ student in Spanish class:

  - Know your material. Make sure you know what you are supposed to be learning!
  - Always do your homework. If you do not understand something, you need to talk to your teacher!
  - Write down pronunciations of words. Writing out how words are pronounced will help you ace that test!
  - Don't get distracted. If something in your Spanish class is distracting you, you will not get an A+ Spanish!
  - Try not to jam too much Spanish into your brain at once! If you have a list of words to memorize, memorize a little at a time!
  - Find someone to practice with you. You'll have fun and you'll learn more than you would in class alone!
  - Make sure you have all of your supplies when you study. It is hard to do an assignment if you don't have your book with you!

SPANISH STUDENT CHECKLIST

Now that we have established a solid foundation for learning Spanish, let's review. Move through this personalized checklist carefully, as it highlights what needs to be done in order to acquire Spanish successfully. And remember—you don't have to do these in order!

____ 1. Recognize any anxious or nervous feelings I may have about learning Spanish.

____ 2. Accept my anxious feelings as normal, ongoing, and part of the learning process.

____ 3. Observe the classroom or place of study carefully, noting the seating arrangement, open spaces, decor, acoustics, and potential distractions.

____ 4. Meet with the instructor about any concerns I have about the classroom setup, and make suggestions if necessary.

____ 5. Assess my teacher's skills by using the *"Qualities of a Great Spanish Teacher"* evaluation form.

____ 6. Show the completed teacher evaluation form to my instructor and share what I like and/or dislike about the program.

____ 7. Evaluate the textbook, workbook, audio CDs, or other components of my language program by doing some research online.

____ 8. Spend extra time thumbing through the textbook, reviewing page appearance, focusing on chapter format, and envisioning the task ahead.

____ 9. Write down any thoughts of dissatisfaction, disappointment, or discouragement related to learning Spanish.

____ 10. Continually read through the encouraging facts about learning Spanish, memorize the shortcuts, and work on developing a more optimistic attitude.

___ 11. Prepare myself, by listing the common listening, speaking, reading, and writing pitfalls that hinder most English speakers who are trying to learn Spanish.

___ 12. Identify what my fears are about trying out my new Spanish skills in front of others.

___ 13. Overcome my fears by not taking the class so seriously, realizing that making mistakes in Spanish can actually be beneficial.

___ 14. Schedule my daily study, review, and practice time weeks ahead, and consistently stick with the program.

___ 15. Stay motivated by rewarding myself for any minor or major accomplishments.

___ 16. Recruit a team of supporters who will encourage me throughout the learning experience.

___ 17. Set a specific proficiency goal and establish a main purpose for learning Spanish.

___ 18. Use the Internet as a Spanish teaching tool and investigate ways it can help me learn more.

___ 19. Follow the suggestions in this guidebook, and experiment with Spanish every chance I get.

___ 20. Sincerely believe that I can learn Spanish today!

I'M GIVING YOU AN A+ IN SPANISH!

After years of teaching Spanish, I've discovered that most students at the intermediate to advanced levels often get frustrated, slow down, or decide to quit. Many end up getting "left behind" simply because one aspect of the language seemed too tough or overwhelming. Hopefully, this guidebook of suggestions has helped eliminate some of the traps, roadblocks, and hindrances that get in your way to learning. Finally, make a note of this page number. These learning tips have helped thousands of Spanish students improve, even during moments when they felt like giving up. So, for those of you who have been following along, I'm giving you an A+ in Spanish. Best of luck and continued success as you learn more about both the Spanish language and the culture of those who speak it. *¡Que te diviertas con tu estudio del español!*

Tu profesor,

Bill Harvey

End-of-Book Spanish Language Practice

TERMINOLOGY

Before you work on your grammar skills, be sure you know the meanings of the words below. They were all presented earlier, so use this list as a quick-reference guide when it's time to practice or review. Notice how the explanations and examples have been simplified for you:

active vs. passive voice: normal subject/verb sentence vs. subject becomes object (e.g., *Ella comió el pan. El pan fue comido por ella.*)

adjective: describes noun and pronoun (e.g., *la niña bonita, yo soy guapo*)

adverb: describes verb, adjective, adverb (e.g., *baila bien, canta profesionalmente*)

affirmative, emphatic, and interrogative: (e.g., *Trabajan. ¡Trabajen! ¿Trabajan?*)

conjugation: [first (*-ar*), second (*-er*), and third (*-ir*)]

consonants: all letters that aren't vowels (e.g., *b, c, d, f,* etc.)

demonstrative: (e.g., *éste, eso, aquella,* etc.)

gender: masculine and feminine (e.g., *el libro, la mesa, el hombre, la mujer*)

imperative mood: (e.g., *¡Vaya a su casa!*)

indicative mood: (e.g., *Ella va a su casa.*)

irregular verb: does not follow the regular conjugation pattern (e.g., present tense—*dar, saber, ir*)

negation: (e.g., *Lo tengo → No lo tengo*)

noun: person, place, thing, or idea (e.g., *amigo, casa, amor*)

number: singular and plural (e.g., *libro—libros, yo—nosotros*)

past participle: most end in *-ado, ido* (e.g., *pintado, servido, visto*)

person: first (*yo, nosotros*), second (*tú, vosotros*), third (*él, ella, Ud., ellos, ellas, Uds.*)

possessive: (e.g., *mi, su, nuestro,* etc.)

preposition: (e.g., *en, para, detrás de,* etc.)

present participle: ends in "-ing" (e.g., *fumando, corriendo, durmiendo*)

pronoun: takes the place of a noun (e.g., *Juan entiende. = Él entiende.*)

reflexive verbs: they have *-se* (e.g., *bañarse, sentarse, despertarse*)

regular verb: follows the regular conjugation pattern (e.g., *hablar, comer, escribir*)

subject, object of a sentence: (e.g., *Juan tiene carro.* Subject is "*Juan,*" object is "*carro*")

subjunctive mood: doubt, desire, emotion, etc. (e.g., *Espero que vaya a su casa.*)

syllable: (e.g., *las par-tes de ca-da pa-la-bra*)

verb infinitive: ends in *–ar, -er,* or *-ir* (e.g., *manejar, beber, salir*)

verb stem and ending: (e.g., *hablamos;* stem is *habl-,* ending is *-amos*)

verb tense : present, past, future, conditional, etc. (e.g., *veo, ví, veré, vería,* etc.)

vowels: (*a, e, i, o, u*)

GRAMMAR DEVELOPMENT

Here's a simple way to improve your grammar. Identify the verb tenses and the parts of speech in each of the following paragraphs. If you want, translate everything into English:

Raúl López trabaja mucho en su hogar. Siempre limpia la casa, lava la ropa y cocina la comida. Vive con su hermano Marcos. Marcos no trabaja. Come todo el día, bebe cerveza y mira televisión. Los dos hermanos son muy diferentes.

Cada lunes, Carla se despierta a las seis. Se baña, se peina y se viste rápido. Ella es enfermera en un hopital grande. Tiene que llegar muy temprano para ayudar al doctor. Carla no duerme mucho porque estudia medicina en la universidad.

Mañana voy a Miami. Visitaré a mis primos en el centro. Vamos a salir en la noche a comer y a bailar a los restaurantes latinos. Estaré con ellos por dos semanas. ¡Será fantástico!

La semana pasada, fui a las montañas con mi familia. Nos divertimos mucho. Dormí bajo las estrellas y vi muchos animales. Mi hermano pescó y mis hermanitas jugaron con nuestro perro. Comimos muy bien. Me gustó mi viaje a las montañas, y quiero volver el próximo año.

Cuando tenía veinte años, Rosa trabajaba en una tienda. Vendía juguetes a los niños. Era una tienda pequeña y siempre venían muchos jóvenes para ver los nuevos juegos, las muñecas y las pelotas. Rosa abría la puerta a las nueve y las cerraba a las seis.

Cada sábado, había una fiesta en la tienda con globos, música y un desfile de juguetes. Rosa era una vendedora excelente porque amaba a los niños.

He tenido una buena vida. Mi esposa y yo hemos vivido los últimos cincuenta años en la misma casa, y ahora tenemos una familia grande aquí en Colorado. Nuestros hijos y nietos nos han ayudado mucho. Nos han lavado la ropa, nos han traído comida y nos han visitado todos los domingos. Creo que he tenido una vida larga porque hemos recibido mucho amor de la familia.

Espero que mi amiga venga mañana. Me alegra que estemos de vacaciones, pero temo que no vaya a llegar temprano. Si ella tuviera un auto nuevo, yo no estaría preocupada. Yo insistía en que tomara el autobús, pero ella quería usar su propio auto. Es muy probable que no tenga ningún problema y que todo salga bien.

READING

Another great way to learn Spanish is to simply read short storybooks or articles. Here's a selection that you should be able to understand, so be sure to complete the five comprehension questions when you finish. By the way, you'll need to check on your answers by yourself!

La cocina latinoamericana
Latin American Cuisine

Un recorrido por México y la América Central y del Sur revela una tremenda selección de ingredientes, sabores y platos culinarios. Las comidas de cada país están representadas por una amplia variedad de orígenes étnicos. Aunque hay un grupo de ingredientes comunes en toda Latinoamérica, la comida de cada país se distingue como resultado de su historia, cultura y gentes.

La historia de la América del Sur le da a sus comidas diversos condimentos, influencias étnicas y métodos de preparación. Por siglos, la gente indígena del continente ha preparado comida como el estofado o como el asado cocidos lentamente sobre el fuego abierto. Pero cuando llegaron los europeos trajeron consigo sus métodos de cocinar. También trajeron una variedad de salsas deliciosas. Por ejemplo, tenemos la influencia española en "el sofrito", uno de los condimentos básicos de la América del Sur, el cual consiste de una mezcla de especias y vegetales que le da a la comida un sabor suave y suculento.

Además de ser una de las comidas latinas más conocidas en Norteamérica, los platos mexicanos también son muy picantes. La gente de México usa cientos de chiles diferentes para sazonar y la comida varía según la región geográfica, dependiendo de los ingredientes que están disponibles. Por esa razón, alguna comida en una parte podría tener el mismo nombre en otra región, pero serían muy diferentes en su condimento y sabor. Por ejemplo, en el norte de México los tamales son preparados con la cáscara del maíz, mientras que en el sur los preparan con la hoja del plátano. Sin embargo, por todo el país las comidas y condimentos básicos son la tortilla, el arroz, los frijoles, el comino, el ajo y los chiles muy picantes.

Las comidas de la América Central son parecidas a las comidas de México y la América del Sur, mezclando la influencia de España con su cultura indígena. Las frutas tropicales y el maní distinguen esta región geográfica de las otras, aunque también guisan con el chile picante. En las zonas interiores de Centroamérica se encuentra más frijoles y nueces, los que normalmente se preparan con la carne de algún animal pequeño. Las zonas de la costa tienen varios pescados y mariscos que se preparan en estofados, asan a la parilla o preparan crudos y encurtidos como el ceviche.

¿Qué es la comida latina? Es una mezcla de culturas, con la influencia de las gentes indígenas combinados con el toque de España, Portugal, Italia y otros países europeos. Hasta la influencia africana se deja degustar en algunos platos latinos. Es decir, la comida latinoamericano es única, colorida, especial, y sobre todo muy sabrosa.

1. Según el ensayo ¿qué trajeron los europeos?
2. ¿Cuáles son algunas comidas típicas de Centroamérica?
3. ¿Qué tipo de comidas preparaban las gentes indígenas?
4. ¿Qué es "el sofrito"?
5. ¿Qué país es conocido por su comida picante?

Mas Práctica
Chapter-by-Chapter Practice Exercises

You can never get enough practice, so here are review exercises from each chapter in the book. The answers are provided below each section:

CHAPTER ONE: THE SOUNDS

A.) Read this list of words aloud:

confiáis   *enfriéis*   *decíais*   *continuéis*   *actuéis*

B.) Continue to pronounce each word correctly:

el general	*el zapato*
el hada	*el queso*
la bondad	*el ñoño*
el guiso	*la victoria*
la vida	*el rastro*

C.) Divide these words into syllables:

1. *nuestro*
2. *reímos*
3. *dieciséis*

4. *ciudad*
5. *viene*

1. *nues-tro*   2. *re-í-mos*   3. *die-ci-séis*   4. *ciu-dad*   5. *vie-ne*

CHAPTER TWO: EXPRESSIONS

A.) Translate these common expressions into Spanish:

1. See you later
2. Happy birthday
3. Thanks a lot
4. Good evening
5. Good luck

6. Merry Christmas
7. Have a nice trip
8. Welcome
9. Get well
10. Happy New Year

1. *Hasta luego*   2. *Feliz cumpleaños*   3. *Muchas gracias*   4. *Buenas noches*   5. *Buena suerte*   6. *Feliz Navidad*   7. *Buen viaje*   8. *Bienvenido*   9. *Que se mejore*   10. *Próspero año nuevo*

B.) Some of these expressions are a bit more difficult. This time, say them in English:

1. *No puede ser.*
2. *Tengo pena.*
3. *¿De verdad?*
4. *No importa.*
5. *Lo siento.*
6. *¡Qué lástima!*
7. *Creo que sí.*
8. *Con razón.*
9. *Por supuesto.*
10. *¡Cómo no!*

1. It can't be.
2. I have grief.
3. Really?
4. It does not matter.
5. I am sorry.
6. What a pity!
7. I think so.
8. No wonder.
9. Of course.
10. Of course!

CHAPTER THREE: VOCABULARY

A.) Translate the following as quickly as you can:

1. *turista*
2. *aniversario*
3. *comunidad*
4. *universidad*
5. *ambicioso*
6. *religioso*
7. *atención*
8. *inteligente*
9. *patriótico*
10. *antiséptico*

1. tourist
2. anniversary
3. community
4. university
5. ambitious
6. religious
7. attention
8. intelligent
9. patriotic
10. antiseptic

B.) Fill in the blanks with the most appropriate question word from the list provided:

1. ¿_____ son tus mejores cursos?   *Cuáles*

2. ¿_____ es su fecha de nacimiento?   *Cuánto*

3. ¿_____ es el dueño de ese carro?   *Qué*

4. ¿_____ hijos tiene Ud.?   *Cómo*

5. ¿_____ fueron los chicos ayer?   *Quién*

6. ¿De _____ nacionalidad son Uds.?   *Dónde*

7. ¿_____ te sientes?   *Adónde*

8. ¿_____ tiempo falta para la boda?   *Cuál*

9. ¿_____ tiene que regresar a su casa?   *Cuántos*

10. ¿_____ está ubicado el teatro?   *Cuándo*

1. ¿*Cuáles* son tus mejores cursos?
2. ¿*Cuál* es su fecha de nacimiento?
3. ¿*Quién* es el dueño de ese carro?
4. ¿*Cuántos* hijos tiene Ud.?
5. ¿*Adónde* fueron los chicos ayer?
6. ¿De *qué* nacionalidad son Uds.?
7. ¿*Cómo* te sientes?
8. ¿*Cuánto* tiempo falta para la boda?
9. ¿*Cuándo* tiene que regresar a su casa?
10. ¿*Dónde* está ubicado el teatro?

C.) Translate the following nouns into Spanish. Some may require both *el* and *la*:

1. French
2. apple
3. victim
4. Thursday
5. potato

6. forehead
7. artist
8. eighteen
9. olive tree
10. champion

1. *el francés, la francesa*
2. *la manzana*
3. *la víctima*
4. *el jueves*
5. *la papa*

6. *la frente*
7. *el/la artista*
8. *el diez y ocho*
9. *el olivo*
10. *el campeón, la campeona*

CHAPTER FOUR: GRAMMAR—PART ONE

A.) Identify the following parts of speech, and then use them in a sentence:

1. *interesante*
2. *para*
3. *nunca*
4. *verde*
5. *ellos*

6. *el pasajero*
7. *allí*
8. *aquellos*
9. *ti*
10. *cubana*

1. adjective (Answers vary)
2. preposition
3. adverb
4. adjective
5. pronoun

6. noun
7. adverb
8. adjective
9. pronoun
10. adjective

B.) Identify the main clause in each of these sentences:

1. *Juana vendía ropa hace años.*
2. *Después de comer, el vendedor barrió la entrada.*
3. *Hablamos con la policía que trabaja en este vecindario.*
4. *Supuestamente Marta y Samuel viven juntos.*
5. *Si tuviera el dinero, me compraría una casa.*
6. *Mientras yo estudiaba, él llamó por teléfono.*
7. *Ella ha viajado con todas sus amigas.*
8. *Quitó la olla del fuego cuando la sopa estaba caliente.*
9. *Durante la clase, escuchamos la música clásica.*
10. *Vamos a repasar el capítulo antes del examen.*

1. *Juana vendía ropa*
2. *el vendedor barrió la entrada*
3. *Hablamos con la policía*
4. *Marta y Samuel viven juntos*
5. *me compraría una casa*

6. *él llamó por teléfono*
7. *Ella ha viajado*
8. *Quitó la olla del fuego*
9. *escuchamos la música clásica*
10. *Vamos a repasar el capítulo*

C.) Use the relative pronoun *que* to combine each pair of sentences below:

1. *Me gusta el postre. El postre es muy dulce.*
2. *Acabo de leer el libro. Me regalaste el libro.*
3. *La señora vivía en la esquina. La señora se murió.*
4. *La niña es mi hija. Ud. vio la niña.*
5. *Ella es la cajera. Ella trabaja conmigo.*
6. *Uso los guantes. Ellos me compraron los guantes.*
7. *Esta es la clase de español. Necesito la clase.*
8. *Llame a los estudiantes. Los estudiantes estudian mucho.*
9. *Tengo algo. Quiero decirte algo.*
10. *Las botellas están en el piso. Las botellas están vacías.*

1. *Me gusta el postre que es muy dulce.*
2. *Acabo de leer el libro que me regalaste.*
3. *La señora que murió vivía en la esquina.*
4. *La niña que usted vió es mi hija.*
5. *Ella es la cajera que trabaja conmigo.*
6. *Uso los guantes que ellos me compraron.*
7. *Esta es la clase de español que necesito.*
8. *Llame a los estudiantes que estudian mucho.*
9. *Tengo algo que quiero decirte.*
10. *Las botellas que están en el piso están vacías.*

D.) Indicate the gender of these nouns correctly by inserting *el* or *la* in front:

1. *disfraz*
2. *mapa*
3. *edad*
4. *cometa*
5. *lodo*
6. *pasaporte*
7. *especie*
8. *pared*
9. *tema*
10. *rubí*
11. *faringitis*
12. *pez*
13. *valor*
14. *cumbre*
15. *jarabe*

1. *el disfraz*
2. *el mapa*
3. *la edad*
4. *el cometa*
5. *el lodo*
6. *el pasaporte*
7. *la especie*
8. *la pared*
9. *el tema*
10. *el rubí*
11. *la faringitis*
12. *el pez*
13. *el valor*
14. *la cumbre*
15. *el jarabe*

E.) Translate the adjective correctly and place it after each noun or nouns.
See example:

1. UGLY　　　　　　*mesas y sillas*　　　　*feas*
2. MODERN　　　　*apartamentos y casas*　　　_____
3. FAT AND SHORT　*conejos*　　　　　　　_____
4. WIDE　　　　　　*calles y caminos*　　　_____
5. RED AND BLUE　　*el único libro*　　　　_____
6. SWEET　　　　　*plátanos y duraznos*　　_____
7. SPANISH　　　　*vendedores y clientes*　_____
8. NEW AND PRETTY　*pantalones*　　　　　_____

9. HAPPY   *muchachas y muchachos* _____

10. DIFFICULT *el otro problema* _____

6. *dulces*
5. *rojo y azul*
4. *anchos*
3. *gordos y bajos*
2. *modernos*

10. *difícil*
9. *felices*
8. *nuevos y bonitos*
7. *españoles*

CHAPTER FIVE: GRAMMAR—PART TWO

A.) Rewrite each sentence with the demonstrative adjective in the plural form. See example:

1. *¿Dónde vive este chico?*   *¿Dónde viven estos chicos?*

2. *Esta silla está rota.* _____

3. *Creo que aquel pájaro es un cuervo.* _____

4. *¿Quién compró esa galleta?* _____

5. *Este carro tiene problemas.* _____

6. *Subieron aquella montaña.* _____

7. *Apagaré esta luz.* _____

8. *¿Cuánto cuesta ese maletín?* _____

9. *Aquel disco compacto no funciona.* _____

10. *Tráigame esa salchicha.* _____

6. *Subieron aquellas montañas.*
5. *Estos carros tienen problemas.*
4. *¿Quién compró esas galletas?*
3. *Creo que aquellos pájaros son cuervos.*
2. *Estas sillas están rotas.*

10. *Tráigame esas salchichas.*
9. *Aquellos discos compactos no funcionan.*
8. *¿Cuánto cuestan esos maletines?*
7. *Apagaré estas luces.*

B.) Replace the subject with the correct subject pronoun. See example:

1. *Toda la clase y yo corríamos.* *Nosotros*

2. *Sandra se fue.* _____

3. *Ud. y Alejandro no pueden entrar.* _____

4. *Mis amigas comen mucho.* _____

5. *San Paulo lo dijo.* _____

6. *El presidente y yo conversamos.* _____

7. *La gente en el cine gritaba.* _____

8. *¿Es española Chila?* _____

9. *Usted y yo hemos tomado café.* _____

10. *Los soldados se perdieron.* _____

3. *Ustedes*   5. *Él*   7. *Ella*   9. *Nosotros*

2. *Ella*   4. *Ellas*   6. *Nosotros*   8. *Ella*   10. *Ellos*

C.) Rewrite each sentence to include a double object pronoun. See example:

1. *Le quiere prestar la escoba a su tía.*   *Quiere prestársela.* _____

2. *Estoy explicando el juego a los niños.* _____

3. *Él te vendía los helados.* _____

4. *Les di el dinero a ellos.* _____

5. *René le trajo papel.* _____

6. *Está mandando los muebles a nosotros.* _____

7. *Les llevé las revistas a Uds.* _____

8. *Ya le bajaron las maletas.* _____

9. *Siempre le hacía el desayuno.* _____

10. *Ella te ha devuelto las joyas.* _____

9. *Siempre se lo hacía.*   5. *René lo trajo.*

8. *Ya se las bajaron.*   4. *Se los di.*

7. *A Uds. se las llevé.*   3. *Él te los vendía.*

10. *Ella te las ha devuelto.*   6. *Nos los está mandando.*   2. *Estoy explicándoselo.*

D.) Fill in the blanks with either *para* or *por*:

1. *Lo escuchamos _____ la radio.*

2. *¿Quiere Ud. tener un auto _____ pasear?*

3. *Vengo _____ decirte que has ganado el premio.*

4. *¡_____ Dios! Ten cuidado con los vasos.*

5. *_____ lo general, suele fumar puros.*

6. *No necesito maletas _____ este viaje.*

7. *Los muebles son _____ Uds.*

8. *_____ tu culpa llegamos tarde.*

9. *Brindamos _____ la feliz pareja.*

10. *Ella estaba paseando _____ la ciudad.*

1. *por*   3. *para*   5. *por*   7. *para*   9. *por*

2. *para*   4. *por*   6. *para*   8. *por*   10. *por*

F.) To practice using adverbs, translate each sentence into English:

1. *No hiciste nada bien.*
2. *Cambió el programa sistemáticamente.*
3. *Limpiaba su cuarto completamente.*
4. *Me habló muy fuerte.*
5. *Llorábamos desesperadamente.*

5. We cried desperately.
4. He spoke to me very firmly.
3. He cleaned his room completely.
2. He changed the program systematically.
1. You didn't do anything well.

CHAPTER SIX: VERBS

A.) Fill in the blank with the present tense form of either *ser* or *estar*.
See example:

1. *Paulo _____ médico.*   <u>Paulo es médico.</u>

2. *El agua en la tina no _____ caliente.*   _____

3. *Ellas _____ las hijas de la señora.*   _____

4. *Nosotros _____ de Cuba.*   _____

5. *¿Dónde _____ la policía?*   _____

6. *Yo _____ un buen estudiante.*   _____

7. *¿Cómo _____ tú hoy día?*   _____

8. *Los hombres _____ en la cocina.*   _____

9. *Yo _____ listo para salir.*   _____

10. *¿Qué hora _____?*   _____

6. *Yo soy un buen estudiante.*
5. *¿Dónde está la policía?*
4. *Nosotros somos de Cuba.*
3. *Ellas son las hijas de la señora.*
2. *El agua en la tina no está caliente.*

10. *¿Qué hora es?*
9. *Yo estoy listo para salir.*
8. *Los hombres están en la cocina.*
7. *¿Cómo estás tú hoy día?*

B.) Change each verb form in the present tense to match the person indicated.
See example:

1. *ponemos*   *(yo)*   <u>*pongo*</u>

2. *viene*   *(nosotros)*   _____

3. *conocen*   *(yo)*   _____

4. *tengo*   *(ellos)*   _____

5. *oímos* (tú) _____

6. *caigo* (ella) _____

7. *venzo* (él) _____

8. *sabemos* (yo) _____

9. *podemos* (ellas) _____

10. *repiten* (nosotros) _____

2. venimos 3. conozco 4. tienen 5. oyes 6. cae 7. vence 8. sé 9. pueden 10. repetimos

C.) *¿Qué pasó ayer?* Follow the model:

1. *organizar la oficina (yo)* — Organicé la oficina ayer.

2. *tocar el piano (él)*

3. *llegar tarde (ellos)*

4. *distribuir los periódicos (tú)*

5. *construir el mueble (ella)*

6. *empezar a estudiar (yo)*

7. *leer la historia (nosotros)*

8. *ver una película (Ud.)*

9. *pagar la cuenta (ellas)*

10. *pescar en el río (Uds.)*

2. Tocó el piano. 3. Llegaron tarde. 4. Distribuiste los periódicos. 5. Construyó el mueble. 6. Empecé a estudiar. 7. Leímos la historia. 8. Vio una película. 9. Pagaron la cuenta. 10. Pescaron en el río.

D.) Complete the translations using either the preterit or the imperfect. See example:

1. They ate the pie last night. — *Anoche ellos comieron el pastel.*

2. She used to wash dishes.

3. We were cleaning the bathroom.

4. Did you wake up at six o'clock?

5. I studied all day long.

6. You guys refused to go.

7. The party lasted six hours. _____

8. Who was living here last year? _____

9. Lincoln was a great president. _____

10. There was an accident on Friday. _____

6. *Ustedes no quisieron ir.*
5. *Estudié todo el día.*
4. *¿Te despertaste a las seis?*
3. *Limpiábamos el baño.*
2. *Ella lavaba los platos.*

10. *Hubo un accidente el viernes.*
9. *Lincoln fue un gran presidente.*
8. *¿Quién vivía aquí el año pasado?*
7. *La fiesta duró seis horas.*

E.) Change each infinitive to the future tense. See example:

1. *Natalia (poner) las flores en el jardín.*   _pondrá_

2. *Los bebitos (dormir) porque tienen sueño.* _____

3. *Yo no (poder) comprar el brazalete.* _____

4. *¿Tú (tomar) todos los refrescos?* _____

5. *La próxima semana Nicolás (empezar) a estudiar.* _____

6. *En la fiesta (haber) un mago.* _____

7. *Algún día nosotros (ser) soldados.* _____

8. *Ellos (estar) en el centro comercial.* _____

9. *¿Cuánto (valer) el carro en dos años?* _____

10. *Yo (hacer) la comida para mañana.* _____

10. *haré*   9. *valdrá*   8. *estarán*   7. *seremos*   6. *habrá*   5. *empezará*   4. *tomarás*   3. *podré*   2. *dormirán*

F.) Change these past tense verbs to the present perfect. See example:

1. *vimos*   _hemos visto_   6. *abrí*   _____

2. *puse*   _____   7. *dijeron*   _____

3. *tenías*   _____   8. *escribiste*   _____

4. *pudieron*   _____ 9. *rompieron*   _____

5. *estaban*   _____   10. *vivíamos*   _____

10. *hemos vivido*   9. *han roto*   8. *has escrito*   7. *han dicho*   6. *he abierto*   5. *han estado*   4. *han podido*   3. *has tenido*   2. *he puesto*

G.) Change these infinitives to the gerund form. See example:

1. caer   *cayendo*   6. sentir _____   11. corregir _____
2. servir _____   7. creer _____   12. leer _____
3. leer _____   8. morir _____   13. medir _____
4. decir _____   9. traer _____   14. dormir _____
5. poder _____   10. oír _____   15. repetir _____

1. cayendo
2. sirviendo
3. leyendo
4. diciendo
5. pudiendo
6. sintiendo
7. creyendo
8. muriendo
9. trayendo
10. oyendo
11. corrigiendo
12. leyendo
13. midiendo
14. durmiendo
15. repitiendo

H.) Change these present tense forms to the conditional. See example:

1. ordeno   *ordenaría*   6. tocan _____
2. crezco _____   7. oigo _____
3. juegan _____   8. es _____
4. vamos _____   9. están _____
5. ves _____   10. aplicas _____

2. crecería
3. jugarían
4. iríamos
5. verías
6. tocarían
7. oiría
8. sería
9. estarían
10. aplicarías

CHAPTER SEVEN: TOUGH TOPICS

A.) Change these dependent noun clauses from the present subjunctive to the imperfect subjunctive. See example:

1. que yo estudie   *que yo estudiara*
2. que él quiera _____
3. que ustedes den _____
4. que tú reconozcas _____
5. que nosotros salgamos _____
6. que ellas tengan _____
7. que Ud. sea _____
8. que yo haga _____

9. *que ellos piensen* _____

10. *que él diga* _____

6. *que ellas tuvieran*
5. *que nosotros saliéramos*
4. *que tú reconocieras*
3. *que ustedes dieran*
2. *que él quisiera*

10. *que él dijera*
9. *que ellos pensaran*
8. *que yo hiciera*
7. *que Ud. fuera*

B.) Write the correct form of the subjunctive on the line provided. See example:

1. *Limpiaron todo antes de que (LLEGAR) mi novia.*   *llegara* _____

2. *Ella lo hace para que nosotros no (TENER) que hacerlo.* _____

3. *El gato vendrá cuando la señora lo (LLAMAR).* _____

4. *Van al desierto aunque (LLOVER).* _____

5. *Practiquen la canción hasta que la (SABER).* _____

6. *Salí sin que Uds. me (DESPEDIR).* _____

7. *Trajo un sombrero en caso de que (SALIR) sol.* _____

8. *Mientras que tú (MENTIR), no te escucharé.* _____

9. *Lo haré a menos que (SURGIR) un problema.* _____

10. *Nosotros no vamos aunque los otros (IR).* _____

6. *despidan*
5. *sepan*
4. *llueva*
3. *llame*
2. *tengamos*

10. *vayan*
9. *surja*
8. *mientas*
7. *salga*

C.) Fill in the blanks with the correct form of the reflexive verb. Use only the present tense:

1. *Juan (quitarse) la camisa y (ponerse) una limpia.*   *se quita, se pone* _____

2. *¿Tú (cepillarse) los dientes después de comer?* _____

3. *Los niños (lavarse) las manos con agua y jabón.* _____

4. *Cuando viajo en barco siempre (marearse).* _____

5. *Nos metemos en calles desconocidas y (perderse).* _____

5. *nos perdemos*
4. *me mareo*

3. *se lavan*
2. *te cepillas*

D.) Use infinitives as you translate these sentences into Spanish:

1. It's possible to swim in the lake.
2. The room is easy to paint.
3. We have to write these words.
4. You (form. sing.) should play tennis.
5. Tell me (inf. sing.) what to do.
6. They have many things to buy.
7. Off to work!
8. Does she know how to pronounce it?
9. It's important to bring the books.
10. I was looking for something to eat.

5. *Dime qué hacer.*
4. *Usted debe jugar tenis.*
3. *Tenemos que escribir estas palabras.*
2. *El cuarto es fácil de pintar.*
1. *Es posible nadar en el lago.*

10. *Estaba buscando algo para comer.*
9. *Es importante traer los libros.*
8. *¿Sabe como pronunciarlo ella?*
7. *¡A trabajar!*
6. *Tienen muchas cosas para comprar.*

E.) Translate these sentences into English:

1. *A ella le falta un cuaderno.*
2. *¿A quién le toca?*
3. *Nos quedan veinte minutos.*
4. *¿Te sobra mucho trabajo?*
5. *A ellos les encanta Nueva York.*
6. *A Ud. le conviene manejar.*
7. *Me interesa ver la película.*
8. *¿No te importa el resultado?*
9. *Nos entusiasmó la conversación.*
10. *A él le gusta patinar solo.*

1. She's missing a notebook.
2. Whose turn is it?
3. We have twenty minutes left.
4. Do you have a lot of work left?
5. They love New York.

6. It would be better for you to drive.
7. I'm interested in seeing the movie.
8. Don't you care about the result?
9. The conversation motivated us.
10. He likes to skate alone.

F.) Change these sentences from the active voice to the passive:

1. *El autor escribió un nuevo libro.*
2. *Nosotros hemos cambiado el número.*
3. *El perro atacará al gato.*
4. *El cartero ha perdido la carta.*
5. *Ellas preparan la comida.*
6. *Delia ama a Raymundo.*
7. *Todos admiran a los soldados.*
8. *La vecina cerró las ventanas.*
9. *Los niños tocarán los instrumentos.*
10. *El camión recoge la basura.*

1. *El nuevo libro fue escrito por el autor.*
2. *El número fue cambiado por nosotros.*
3. *El gato será atacado por el perro.*
4. *La carta ha sido perdida por el cartero.*
5. *La comida es preparada por ellas.*

6. *Raymundo es amado por Delia.*
7. *Los soldados son admirados por todos.*
8. *Las ventanas fueron cerradas por la vecina.*
9. *Los instrumentos serán tocados por los niños.*
10. *La basura es recogida por el camión.*